KENYA

KENYA

BY LAUREL CORONA

LUCENT BOOKS
P.O. BOX 289011
SAN DIEGO, CA 92198-9011

Library of Congress Cataloging-in-Publication Data

Corona, Laurel, 1949–
    Kenya / by Laurel Corona.
        p.   cm. — (Modern nations of the world)
    Includes bibliographical references (p.   ) and index.
    Summary: Examines the land, people, history, and culture of
Kenya and discusses its state of affairs and place in the world today.
    ISBN 1-56006-590-7 (lib. bdg. : alk. paper)
    1. Kenya Juvenile literature. [1. Kenya.] I. Title.
II. Series.
  DT433.522.C67 2000
  967.62—dc21
                                                                     99-25321
                                                                       CIP

Copyright © 2000 by Lucent Books, Inc.
P.O. Box 289011, San Diego, CA 92198-9011
Printed in the U.S.A.

CONTENTS

INTRODUCTION

A VIBRANT NATION

In 1911 a German entymologist looking for insect specimens along the border between Kenya and Tanzania slipped and fell into a deep gorge. Scratched and bruised but otherwise unhurt, Professor Kattwinkil began to look around. What he saw would forever change humanity's understanding of human history. Surrounding him in the Olduvai Gorge were fossils that looked curiously human but had to be several million years old.

His discovery began one of the great scientific quests of the century. Years of painstaking work by scientists at this site and others in Kenya would support the theory that the cradle of humankind is eastern Africa. This theory suggests that every person on Earth is at least remotely related to those original Africans.

East Africa may have been the center of human life in the past, but it has been largely overlooked by the Western world in the last few decades. Since the end of Africa's colonial period in the 1960s, any information about the continent on the evening news in the United States is likely to be only the latest famine, disease, ethnic violence, or military coup. These things are all part of the reality of modern Africa, to be sure, but they do not form the whole picture.

KENYAN KALEIDOSCOPE

Kenya has not only an astonishing past but also a vibrant present. In Mombasa harbor a small Swahili dhow sails in the shadows of an incoming cruise ship, which is carrying passengers bound for an inland safari, and an outbound freighter, which is loaded with coffee beans headed for European or Asian ports. On the inland savannas tourists snap pictures while a giraffe languidly crosses the road, bending its neck to pass under the telephone wires. In the highlands a Kikuyu girl weeds around young coffee plants on her family's small farm while only a few miles away, but several thousand feet lower, a young Maasai helps his father tend cattle in the Rift Valley. Farther up the valley, a community erecting a new hospital stops work so that the local elder can perform the traditional invocation of the god Ngai. On the rutted dirt road near the border with Somalia, travelers bounce painfully on the wooden seats of the only available transportation, an old truck whose bed has been converted into seating for paying passengers. The air is hot and dry, but in several hours they will be in a rain forest at the top of the mountain they see looming from the desert floor.

Outside Nairobi, a lion brings down a gazelle within sight of skyscrapers. In those skyscrapers an adviser to the president of Kenya is negotiating the financial terms for permitting a dam to be built or a foreign corporation to sell its products in Kenya. In Parliament a speaker is shouted down for accusing the president of illegal practices. Across town a new school named for the president is being ceremonially opened while a few blocks away a youth is arrested for distributing

The city of Nairobi represents the merging of modern life and traditional cultures that make up Kenya today.

AFRICA

pamphlets about an opposition party's upcoming rally for constitutional reform. In one of the cities a woman mayor bangs her gavel; meanwhile, in a private hut only a mile away, a young girl's genitals are being mutilated to make her more marriageable when she grows up.

GROWING PAINS

Kenya is clearly a place of extreme contrasts—the pleasing and the unsavory, the old and the new. Forty years ago the nation of Kenya did not exist. Fifty years ago Africans living in present-day Kenya were shot or imprisoned for their efforts to gain freedom from a white colonial government. Not

much more than one hundred years ago, most of these same
Africans had never even seen a white face. It has been a tu-
multuous century. The legacy of white intervention in Africa,
combined with African Kenyans' accelerated pace of change
from traditional to modern ways, has not created a smooth
path for Kenya as it moves into the twenty-first century. The
way to have the best—and avoid the worst—of both traditional and modern cultures has been no easier for Kenya to
figure out than it has for any other modernizing nation. Even
still, most observers see Kenya as a bright star on the African
continent. According to Blaine Harden, the former sub-
Saharan bureau chief for the *Washington Post*, Kenya has
"the best port, the best roads, the best climate, the best work
force, the best communications network, the best international reputation, and the most vigorous free market tradition in East Africa."[1] As a modern nation, Kenya is a place of
tremendous opportunity with a rich cultural heritage on
which to build.

1

THE LAND

It is hard to imagine a place more varied in appearance than Kenya. Divided in half by the equator, its 224,961 square miles make it slightly smaller than Texas, but within that area a person can travel from undersea coral reefs to the top of the second highest peak in Africa. A person can travel from a region so hot and dry that laundry is stiff after ten minutes on a clothesline to emerald green jungles where rain falls for days at a time. A person can travel from salty desert lakes, which are home to thousands of giant fish and crocodiles, to forests where monkeys chatter in trees and then to lakes where flamingos are so numerous that the water seems to be painted pink. A person can stand on the edge of a huge tear in the surface of the earth and look down thousands of feet to where Maasai herdsmen follow their cattle, or one can look across endless expanses of savanna where lions prowl and tourists on safari stop to shoot—now only with cameras. As author Michael Maren points out, "Within Kenya's borders are nearly every type of landscape found on planet Earth."[2]

LOCATION AND NEIGHBORS

Kenya is located in East Africa. It shares its northern border with Sudan and Ethiopia. Farther northwest are the sands of the Sahara; the arid conditions of northern Kenya are caused by the same climatic forces that created that huge desert. Kenya's western border includes Lake Victoria and Uganda. To the south, the Serengeti Plain, which is famous for its wildlife, spills over into Kenya from Tanzania. Likewise, Tanzania's Mount Kilimanjaro, the highest peak in Africa, is clearly visible in southern Kenya and forms part of the overall landscape. Kenya is bordered to the east by Somalia and the Indian Ocean. Its coastline is protected by a barrier reef, which creates calm turquoise blue water and sandy beaches.

In Kenya, as elsewhere around the world, climate is directly affected by altitude. Most people associate equatorial lands with thick tropical rain forests, but very little of Kenya is actually jungle. Even though it straddles the equator, most

Mount Kilimanjaro, the highest peak in Africa.

of Kenya is too high for tropical vegetation to grow. To the west of Kenya, where the elevation is lower, the vast, nearly impenetrable rain forests of the Congo basin begin to dominate the landscape.

THE HIGHLANDS

In the southwest corner of Kenya is a region known as the highlands, where elevations range from three thousand to ten thousand feet. Living here is easier than in other parts of Kenya and much of Africa because of the generally mild weather; thus, this part of Kenya is one of the most densely populated rural areas of the world. About 80 percent of Kenya's population lives in this area. A map of Kenya shows this concentration of population; most of the towns and cities are located in this region. It is here, about three hundred miles from the coast, that the capital, Nairobi, is located.

The highlands are a large plateau taking up approximately 25 percent of the land mass of Kenya. Unlike many plateaus, however, the land here is not flat. The highlands are quite hilly and are broken up by several mountain ranges; an extraordinary chasm, the Great Rift Valley; and Mount Kenya. On the plateau itself are large expanses of cultivated land, but much of the land is still wild; lions, zebras, rhinoceroses, giraffes, and baboons are common sights. The climate of the highlands is varied, according to the altitude and other factors. At higher elevations temperatures can reach freezing.

Lions, rhinoceroses, and zebras roam freely in the highlands of Africa.

Other parts of the higher mountains are covered with bamboo thickets, and in some areas it rains heavily. At lower altitudes the climate is temperate. It is generally drier at the lower elevations of the plateau, except for two annual rainy seasons, which may produce up to forty inches of rainfall.

The Ngong Hills, located south of Nairobi, are a particularly beautiful part of Kenya. It is here that Isak Dinesen, the author of *Out of Africa*, lived. The local ethnic group, the Maasai, describe these hills as having been created when a giant tripped over Mount Kilimanjaro. When he fell, his knuckles carved out the distinctive shape of the hills.

It is easy to see why so many people, including Europeans who came in the nineteenth century to colonize Kenya, would want to live in the Kenya highlands. Not only is the weather pleasant and the scenery and wildlife spectacular, but the soil is also rich, and the growing season is long enough to cultivate a variety of crops. "A more charming region is not to be found in all Africa,"[3] declared one colonial explorer, Joseph Thompson, in the 1880s.

ISAK DINESEN

One of the best-known European colonists in Kenya was Karen Blixen, who wrote under the pen name Isak Dinesen. Her memoirs, *Out of Africa*, were made into a film starring Meryl Streep and Robert Redford. The memoirs detail her years in the Ngong Hills just south of Nairobi. Although, according to Dennis Boyles, author of *African Lives*, "her attitude toward Africans . . . was conditional, convenient, vividly patronizing and no doubt deeply offensive to both the white and native communities," she wrote very detailed, loving, and beautiful descriptions of her surroundings. The following passages are from *Out of Africa*, which she wrote years after returning to her native Denmark.

There is always something magnanimous about elephants. To follow a rhino into own country is hard work; the space that he clears in the thorn-thicket is just a few inches too low for the hunter, and he will have to keep his head bent a little all the time. The elephant on his march through dense forest calmly tramples out a green fragrant tunnel, lofty like the nave of a cathedral.

. . . .

The sight of a lion goes straight to the heart. . . . Going back into the past I do, I believe, remember each individual lion I have seen—his coming into the picture, his slow raising or rapid turning of his head, the strange snakelike swaying of his tail. "Praise be to thee, Lord, for Brother Lion, the which is very calm, with mighty paws, and flows through the red grass, red-mouthed, silent, with the roar of the thunder ready in his chest."

. . . .

You have tremendous views as you get up above the African highlands [in a plane], surprising combinations and changes of light and colouring, the rainbow on the green sunlit land, the gigantic upright clouds and big wild black storms, all swing round you in a race and a dance. . . . When you have flown over the Rift Valley and the volcanoes of Suswa and Longonot, you . . . have been to the lands on the other side of the moon. You may at other times fly low enough to see the animals on the plains and to feel toward them as God did when he had just created them, and before he commissioned Adam to give them names. . . . Every time I have gone up in an aeroplane and looking down have realized I was free of the ground, I have had the consciousness of a great new discovery. "I see:" I have thought, "This was the idea. And now I understand everything."

European colonist Karen Blixen wrote Out of Africa *under the pen name Isak Dinesen.*

THE HIGHLAND MOUNTAINS

Rising above the lower elevations of the plateau are the Nyandarua Mountains (also called the Aberdare Mountains after Lord Aberdare, head of the Royal Geographic Society during the colonial period) and the Mau Escarpment. These two ranges run north to south and average around ten thousand feet in elevation. The Aberdares are one of the many national parks of Kenya, although they are not as frequently visited as some other parks because weather and poor roads make travel difficult. The Mau range is even less visited, as are the several other escarpments in the area. Both the Aberdares and the escarpments have large pastures and thick forests and are home to several of the ethnic groups of Kenya, including the Kikuyu, Kenya's largest group.

Among Kenya's many national parks is Aberdare, where the magnificent Magura Falls can be found.

Towering even above the mountain ranges are Mount Kenya and Mount Elgon. Mount Kenya rises to over seventeen thousand feet, only surpassed in elevation by one other

mountain in Africa, Mount Kilimanjaro in neighboring Tanzania. The equator runs directly across Mount Kenya, whose perennially snowcapped peaks produce an interesting anomaly: It is possible to have a snowball fight on the equator! Mount Kenya is a 3 1/2 million-year-old volcano. On the northern side of Mount Kenya are large meadows where wheat is grown. The topography is rougher on the south and east sides, with many gorges and mountain ridges. Kenyan coffee, acknowledged to be some of the world's best, is grown on terraced hills in this area and other parts of the highlands. Like Mount Kenya, Mount Elgon is also an extinct volcano. It is located on the Ugandan border. There are a number of lava tube caves in Mount Elgon, and the salt deposits in these caves attract elephants. It is now believed that some of the caves may actually have been created by elephants who, over eons of time, broke off the rock with their tusks in order to lick the salt.

THE GREAT RIFT VALLEY

Running between the Aberdare Mountains and the Mau Escarpment is the Great Rift Valley. Beginning in southwest Asia and crossing parts of the Middle East, the valley cuts through Africa, crosses Kenya, and ends in the Indian Ocean beyond Mozambique. The Red Sea north of Kenya, which separates Africa from the Middle East, is part of the rift. The rift is the result of shifts in the earth's surface caused by two land masses known as tectonic plates. Volcanoes are often associated with action along the edges of tectonic plates, and this accounts for the presence of so many volcanic peaks in Kenya.

In Kenya, the floor of the Great Rift Valley is not actually low in elevation. It can be as high as six thousand feet, which, if the surrounding land were at or near sea level, would constitute a mountain or high plateau. However, in the highlands of Kenya there may be as much as a three-thousand-foot drop between the plateau and the Rift Valley floor. In many places the canyon walls are almost vertical, as in the Grand Canyon in Arizona. The width of the Great Rift Valley varies, but in parts it is forty miles wide. The Maasai bring their herds of cattle into the Rift Valley to graze.

Workers pick coffee beans on the terraced hills of Kenya's highlands.

Flamingos stop at Lake Nakuru in search of food.

Lakes are strung out like sparkling stones on a bracelet along the Great Rift Valley. Lake Nakuru, one hundred miles from Nairobi, is particularly noteworthy. More than a million flamingos stop over on its shores during their migration to eat algae from the lake. When the flamingos take off from Lake Nakuru, the sound of their wings can be heard for miles. These flamingos are only one of several hundred bird species on Lake Nakuru.

THE WESTERN PLATEAU AND LAKE VICTORIA

On the western side of the highlands, the land drops towards the basin that forms Lake Victoria. As the elevation drops, the temperature rises. This westernmost part of Kenya is hot year round and has high humidity and substantial rainfall, particularly in the evenings—a typical weather pattern in equatorial regions of the world. Although the land is rocky and mountainous and therefore difficult to farm, maize, millet, cotton, and rice are all produced in the area, and cattle and goats are grazed here. Most of Kenya's tea and sugarcane also comes from this area. The western plateau is home to the

Luo, the second most influential ethnic group in Africa, many of whom make a living fishing on Lake Victoria.

Lake Victoria is Africa's largest lake and the second largest on Earth; only Lake Superior is larger. The lake itself is bigger than many countries. In fact, it is almost the size of the whole country of Ireland. Lake Victoria is called Victoria Nyanza by Kenyans. On the shores of Lake Victoria is Kisumu, the third largest city in Kenya, after Nairobi and the port of Mombasa. At one time Kisumu was an important trade link

---

THE NANDI BEAR AND LITTLE RED MEN

In many areas of the world where humans live on the edge of nearly impenetrable tracts of land, legends arise about mysterious creatures who are seen only fleetingly or are known only by tracks or other signs they leave behind. Well-known examples are the abominable snowman, or yeti, in the Himalayas; and bigfoot, or Sasquatch, in the Pacific Northwest. In Africa there are other examples.

The Nandi bear is said to live in the Nandi Hills of western Kenya, between Nairobi and Lake Victoria. One theory is that it was a real creature around which legends were built, but it is now extinct. Others insist that it lives today and point to mutilated livestock as evidence. Called Chemoset by the Nandi, it is claimed to resemble a large dog, bear, or ape. If it exists, it is most likely a large creature such as a gorilla. However, no gorillas have ever been seen in the Nandi Hills. The dead livestock is more likely to have been killed by leopards. Opinion is deeply divided over whether the Nandi bear is fact or fiction.

In the hills around Meru, just east of Mount Kenya, live the Mbere people, who are related to the Kikuyu. The Mbere, particularly the elderly, are believed to possess magical powers. The origins of these powers are either secret or forgotten, but the Mbere believe that there is a link between their magic and the existence in the Meru Hills of red men approximately four feet tall, to whom they are somehow related. Anthropologists once hoped, however unrealistically, that these little red men might be surviving hominids, but no solid evidence that they exist has ever been found. The Mbere point to mysterious fires in the hills that brought on rain in a recent drought as evidence that the little red men are real and are trying to help the Mbere survive.

between the interior of equatorial Africa (accessible primarily by water) and the coast (accessible from Kisumu by train). Modern times have brought more and better roads, and Kisumu's role as a trade center has shrunk. Its role was further reduced in the 1980s by political upheavals in Uganda and other neighboring countries, which disrupted the economies of those countries and thus affected their ability to export goods. Kisumu is now a fairly quiet city.

THE EASTERN PLATEAU AND THE GAME RESERVES

Probably everyone has seen pictures of at least one part of Kenya. In these pictures, lions stalk gazelles, huge herds of wildebeest thunder in a cloud of dust, rhinos face down tourist vehicles, zebras gather at the water holes, and giraffes and elephants stroll leisurely between small stands of trees. The backdrop for all these familiar images is the African savanna.

The term *savanna* is used to describe wide open expanses of grassland in Africa. In the United States the equivalent term is *plains*. The savanna is dry most of the year—too dry to cultivate successfully—although some attempts are now being made because of the increasing population of Kenya. The soil is rocky, and vegetation, except immediately around sources of water, is mostly scattered brush such as acacia

An elephant safari in the Maasai Mara National Reserve.

and thorn trees. The most unusual plant on the savanna is the baobab. It is generally no taller than a two-story house, but because it uses the trunk to store water, it can be as wide as thirty to fifty feet in diameter. A large baobab tree may be up to two thousand years old.

The eastern plateau varies in elevation but averages around three thousand feet. It has two regions roughly divided by the Tana River, which runs eastward through much of the region before heading south to the coast. North of the Tana the climate becomes progressively hotter and dryer. Kenya becomes desert as it nears the borders of Somalia and Ethiopia.

The region south of the Tana experiences a short but substantial rainy season, which accounts for the typical savanna vegetation and wildlife. This is where the largest game reserve, the Tsavo National

Storing water in its trunk, a baobab tree can be as wide as fifty feet at its base.

Park, is located. It is the size of the state of Massachusetts. Farther west, not actually in the eastern plateau but in a geographically similar region south of Nairobi, is the Amboseli National Park, another reserve; and the Serengeti Plain, where the Maasai Mara National Reserve is located. Most of the Serengeti is actually in Tanzania. The Amboseli National Park is known not only for its game but also for its thirty-eight square mile lake that appears in the rainy season but goes totally dry in the summer. A little northeast of Nairobi is the Meru National Park, another game reserve. The story of Elsa, the lioness from the book and movie *Born Free*, took place in the Meru National Park.

THE NORTHERN DESERT

The old Northern Frontier District (still called the NFD by some) is a sparsely populated, lightly traveled area. Most Kenyans know and think little if anything about it, and it is rarely visited by tourists. The Somali border is an arbitrary one and is easily crossed, and the ethnic hostilities that recently caused war in Somalia often spill over into northern Kenya. The area has no particularly strong ethnic ties to the rest of Kenya, and most of its people are of Somali or Ethiopian origin. The area is crisscrossed with migration routes but few permanent roads. The two main landmarks of this area are Lake Turkana, which extends down into Kenya's Chalbi Desert from the Ethiopian border, and Mount Marsabit.

LAKE TURKANA

Until place names were "Kenyanized" in the 1970s, Lake Turkana was known as Lake Rudolf. It was named after Archduke Rudolf of Austria, who financed the expedition that resulted in Europeans' first view of this, the largest permanent desert lake in the world. Lake Turkana's shoreline is more extensive than the whole Kenya coast, but unlike that area, its shores are almost completely unpopulated. Lake Turkana is

NORWEGIAN FISHERMEN ON LAKE TURKANA?

In the 1970s, as Western nations pondered how to help the newly independent nations of Africa, the Norwegian government saw Lake Turkana as a resource that was going to waste. The Turkana people did not even eat fish from the lake, but instead kept to their nomadic lifestyle, subsisting on their herds. The Norwegians thought they had found a way to improve the lives of the Turkana by creating an exportable commodity and a new food source.

They brought a fishing trawler to the small lakeshore town of Kalokol and built a fish filleting and freezing plant. Many Turkana were persuaded to give up their nomadic lifestyles and move to the lake, but others simply brought their herds and left them to graze, wreaking ecological havoc on the surrounding area. But this was the least dramatic of the problems. After two days it became obvious that the electrical supply was insufficient to run the freezers. In fact, it would have taken more electrical power than was available in all of northern Kenya. The fish rotted, and the area was too remote to make exporting fresh fish possible. Soon after, the trawler sank. While the Norwegians and the Kenyan government were figuring out what to do next, an irrigation project to the north in Ethiopia diverted water from the lake and the shoreline began to recede, leaving the plant surrounded today by desert, a mile or more from the shore.

less remote than it used to be because of attempts to establish commercial ventures, but so far these attempts have not been very successful. It is on the shores of Lake Turkana that anthropologist Richard Leakey unearthed some of the oldest fossil evidence of early humans.

Lake Turkana is actually smaller now than at any other point in known history. The Nile River used to feed into this huge inland sea, which accounts for the huge Nile perch (the record is 238 pounds) which live in the lake. Lake Turkana is located in the middle of miles of rocky outcroppings and sand, and it fascinates its few visitors by its many changes of color in the course of a day—from jade green to turquoise to milky blue to gray. It is filled by runoff, but it has no outlet. Evaporation has made it notably salty and alkaline. As on the Great Salt Lake in Utah, swimmers would bob on its surface without sinking because of its high salt and mineral content, but few swimmers venture onto Lake Turkana because of the thousands of Nile crocodiles that sun themselves in large piles on its banks. Hippopotamuses also live here, although they are rarely seen.

MOUNT MARSABIT

Rising above the desert in northeastern Kenya is an extinct volcano called Mount Marsabit. From miles away, travelers across the desert can see the permanently lush and green vegetation on its slopes. It is no wonder that this landmark, and particularly the oasis town of Marsabit near the crater, became a trading center for nomads. In the center of Marsabit, people dressed in the colorful ethnic costumes mingle to rest and do business before returning to the desert floor below. Occasionally elephants wander into town, creating havoc among the merchants.

Mist and clouds cover the top of Mount Marsabit, and it rains nearly every day. The two craters on the peak of Mount Marsabit are filled with water. Travelers sometimes see long-tusked elephants drinking the water in the crater, but the vines and thick vegetation, as well as the cobras, make it difficult to get down to the lakes to get a closer look.

THE KENYA COAST

The Kenya coast looks like the tropical paradise of imagination. The coast is lined with sandy beaches and lagoons and is spotted with offshore islands. Coconut palms sway in the breeze that comes in across the turquoise water. A coral reef breaks up the ocean waves and calms the water along the beaches as well as provides a home for many species of fish and other underwater life. The Kenya coast is a dream come true for beach lovers, snorkelers, and scuba divers, and it has become a major resort destination.

Others come to the coast of Kenya for another reason. Mombasa is the port for all cargo and cruise ships doing business in Kenya. Many tourists stay here only briefly before heading inland on safari, but many others have recognized that the Kenya coast is a destination in itself because of its interesting Swahili culture and natural beauty. The Kenya coast, though not extensive, is therefore an important part of the country's economy and history.

MOMBASA

Palm trees provide shade on the south coast of Mombasa.

Mombasa is the second largest city in Kenya, and it is far more historically interesting than Nairobi. Mombasa is actually an island at the opening of a large natural harbor. There

has been a town here continually for over seven hundred years, and evidence exists of other civilizations as far back as two thousand years. Here, Arabs intermingled with indigenous African groups to produce the Swahili culture and the kiSwahili language. Today a few Swahili-style boats, called dhows, still ply the harbor and coastal waters along with large freighters and sleek cruise liners, and in the old town itself are narrow lanes, mosques, and public squares that clearly show the historic mixing of Islamic and African cultures.

Kenya's second largest city, Mombasa, is the cradle of the Swahili culture.

THE COASTLINE

To the south and north of Mombasa are coastal stretches of beach broken up by mangrove swamps and rivers and streams that tumble or meander down to the ocean from their inland sources. This coastal area is more junglelike than most other parts of Kenya. Many species of monkeys, birds, and butterflies make their homes in this narrow coastal strip. Besides relaxation in the sun, archaeology is a main interest of many who come to the Kenya coast. Many ruined mosques, forts, and even whole towns have been cleared from the ever-encroaching vegetation, and a few vibrant island towns give fascinating glimpses into the life of eastern coastal Africa hundreds of years ago.

The island of Lamu is known for its archaeological sites and its anachronistic charm.

Besides Mombasa, the best-known island is Lamu, located near the Somali border. Archaeological sites here are at least twelve hundred years old. Electricity came to Lamu only about thirty years ago, and there is only one road; no other roads are needed because there is only one car, and it is owned by the Kenyan government. For all other travel there are donkeys and the travelers' own two feet. Lamu and the surrounding islands are hot and dry much of the year and hot and humid the rest. Lamu has become a popular tourist destination precisely because of its anachronistic charm, its mix of cultures, and its sense of long history.

Given the amazing range of environments in Kenya, it is easy to understand why so many different ethnic cultures, traditions, and ways of life have evolved. It is also easy to see why Kenya has interested such a broad range of outsiders. Many foreigners, particularly first-time visitors, are attracted to Kenya because of its large game and other wildlife, but when they take the time, their interest often becomes lifelong because of the country's beauty, history, and human diversity.

THE PEOPLE

In Kenya there are over forty African ethnic groups in addition to Europeans and Asians, who together comprise only about 2 percent of the population. Relationships among the groups generally depend on two things: proximity and language. Groups whose ancestral lands are close to each other have more opportunity to interact, and are likely to have more in common—and, unfortunately, more potential for hostility. And clearly, groups who can understand each other's language are more apt to be drawn together either by a sense of kinship, however remote, or by the sheer convenience of being mutually understood.

An example of the effects of proximity and language is in northern Kenya, where residents only reluctantly acknowledge themselves as citizens of Kenya. The land is generally suited only to a nomadic lifestyle. Groups such as the Somali and Galla, who live in northern Kenya, do not pay much attention to national borders and are more closely tied ethnically and linguistically to Somalia and Ethiopia—and to each other—than to the rest of Kenya.

Population counts to determine the size of Kenya's different ethnic groups are often inaccurate because some groups, like the Maasai, refuse to cooperate and because tribes intermingle more than they used to. Still, there is no doubt that the largest and most powerful group is the Kikuyu. The Luo and the Luhya are second and third in size, though there is some question as to the order. Undoubtedly, the Luo are the second most powerful and important both presently and historically. Among the other ethnic groups in Kenya, the Maasai stand out as perhaps the most mythical and colorful. Other smaller but particularly notable groups include the Somalis and the Turkana along the northern border and the Kalenjin in the Great Rift Valley.

THE KIKUYU

The Kikuyu (the closest pronunciation is "Gekoyo") are the largest, wealthiest, and most powerful African group in Kenya. Their ancestral home is the highlands of Kenya, including

RICHARD LEAKEY

Although white Kenyans make up less than 2 percent of the population of Kenya today, some of them are very influential. In the first part of his life, Richard Leakey was best known for his famous parents and his own discoveries of fossils in the Lake Turkana area. In 1989 Leakey began another career when, at President Moi's request, he took over as director of the Kenya Wildlife Service (KWS). Moi was concerned about the near extinction of rhinoceroses and elephants in Kenya's game reserves due to poaching, and he gave Leakey wide latitude to turn the situation around. Under Leakey's direction, antipoaching units were legally permitted to kill poachers on sight, and tracts of Maasai land were declared off limits to humans, including the Maasai. These radical solutions worked for the rhinos and elephants, whose populations began to grow again, but they were considered too drastic by many Kenya residents, particularly the Maasai.

In June 1993 Leakey's private plane crashed, and he lost both of his legs. Undaunted, he learned to use artificial limbs. By the time he returned to work, however, the political climate had changed, and he found himself charged with corruption and mismanagement of the KWS. In fact, Leakey was disliked because he would not go along with the normal corrupt practices of government service, and it was probably his refusal to go along with graft that got him accused of it. His downfall at KWS was in part caused by his prickly personality, and in part by a concerted effort by some Maasai to get rid of him. He resigned in embarrassment.

In May 1995 he decided to enter politics and petitioned to establish a new political party. It came as no surprise that the petition was refused by Moi; Leakey's stated purpose for establishing the new party was his dissatisfaction with Moi's leadership. Moi, he felt, had mismanaged Kenya, corrupted public service, and eroded the overall quality of life. Moi countered, calling Leakey a racist colonial. Leakey continues to speak out against Moi and to antagonize many other Kenyans, but there is no doubt that as an anthropologist and as an environmentalist he has made important contributions to the only country he has ever called home.

Richard Leakey has made important contributions as an anthropologist and director of Kenya's wildlife service.

The Kikuyu are the largest, wealthiest, and most powerful ethnic group in Kenya's highlands.

Mount Kenya itself, where they have farmed for centuries. The Kikuyu, as well as many other agriculturalists, were polygamous. They began the custom of increasing the number of wives available to them by paying "bride prices," essentially a fee for taking a woman away from her own community. They also cleared forests and planted crops on the highlands, giving the local hunter-gatherers some of the harvest in exchange for use of the land.

Through intermarriage, trade, and other cultural intermingling, the Kikuyu gradually became the dominant group in the highlands. This pattern of bringing neighboring hunter-gatherers or nomadic people into agricultural cultures is common, and it is the main way, other than by warfare, that one group comes to dominate an area.

The Kikuyu had a less peaceful relationship with the Maasai of the Great Rift Valley area, who often raided the Kikuyu's herds of cattle. Raids and counterraids were, ironically, the way in which strong links were made between these two tribes. Resolving conflict became a reason for the two groups to interact, and in the process they came to respect each other, to trade, to intermarry, and to adopt some of each other's cultural traditions. Many of the practices of the Kikuyu, such as structuring community life around age groups, are actually borrowed from the Maasai, although the Maasai themselves appear to have originally borrowed this idea from the Kalenjin, another Rift Valley group.

The prominence of the Kikuyu in Kenya today is largely a result of colonial settlement in the highlands. The Kikuyu were the most harmed by colonialism because it was their land that was most prized by the settlers and their culture most disrupted. However, their proximity also put them in a position to gain the most by association with the colonists. The Kikuyu had more opportunities for higher education and to observe how modern bureaucracies, businesses, and governments operate. Thus, their location in the Nairobi area and in the well-developed surrounding highlands put them in the best position to move into the forefront of Kenyan politics when Kenya became independent in 1963. The first president of Kenya, Jomo Kenyatta, was a Kikuyu.

The Kikuyu's initial role in the forefront of independent Kenya was well deserved for another reason. It was within

KENYAN ETHNIC GROUPS

SUDAN

ETHIOPIA

Turkana

Lake Turkana

Mandera

Moyale

Somali

El Molo

UGANDA

Boran

Marsabit

Wajir

Pokot

Rendille

Somali

Luhya

Kalenjin

Samburu

SOMALIA

Mt. Elgon

Mt. Kenya

Isiolo

Luo

Meru

Nandi

Nakuru

Lake Victoria

Luo

Embu

Kikuyu

Tana River

Gusii

Nairobi

Galla

Machakos

Maasai

Kamba

Giriama

TANZANIA

Taveta

Indian Ocean

Voi

Taita

Swahili

Malindi

Mombasa

the Kikuyu that the movement to over-throw colonialism was most strongly rooted. In the 1920s the Kikuyu began to organize politically, and by the 1930s they had set up Kikuyu Independent Schools. The British had been reluctant to teach Africans English because of the belief that if Africans could not speak the language of those in power, they could not become powerful themselves. In frustration, the Kikuyu opened their own schools to teach their children English. Later, in the 1950s, the Kikuyu were at the heart of the Mau Mau rebellion, an underground move-ment to overthrow the colonial govern-ment. Thousands of Kikuyu were killed or imprisoned during that period. Many of the villages in which Kikuyu live today got their start as internment centers. In the town of Nyeri, the center of Kikuyuland, a monument that reads, "To the Memory of the Members of the Kikuyu Tribe Who Died in the Fight for Freedom 1951–1957," serves as a constant reminder of this era.

Jomo Kenyatta, a Kikuyu, was the first president of Kenya.

Nyeri, north of Nairobi, was a preestablished market town that grew as a hub for the marketing of coffee and other goods from the colonial plantations. The Nyeri area is now divided into many *shambas*, or small farms, and is the most com-pletely cultivated area in Kenya. During the colonial era the Kikuyu were forced onto less arable lands, which they suc-ceeded in cultivating. Then, after independence, the large colonial plantations were divided up and given back to the Africans. These two factors, plus the overall fertility and good growing weather of the area, have made it a prosperous part of Kenya. The area's economy, though almost exclusively agri-cultural, is still more broad based than in many other areas of Kenya because a wider variety of crops, including maize, beans, potatoes, bananas, sugarcane, millet, squash, melons, citrus fruit, macadamia nuts, tea, and coffee, are grown there.

The Kikuyu are the most powerful group in Kenya, but there are rivalries among them. These rivalries stem from dif-ferences of opinion about the best future direction for Kenya, as well as a desire to be the group that comes out on top, no matter what direction Kenya takes. In recent years a political schism has arisen between two branches of the Kikuyu, the Nyeri Kikuyu and the Kiambu Kikuyu, Jomo Kenyatta's group, who live around Kiambu on the northern outskirts of Nairobi.

IRON FROM SAND

In his 1938 book *Facing Mount Kenya*, Jomo Kenyatta, the future first president of Kenya, described traditional Kikuyu life, including the way the Kikuyu turned sand into iron. The practice probably has not changed much since the Iron Age and illustrates both the ingenuity and the difficulty of the undertaking.

As Kenyatta tells it, ore-bearing sand is gathered and the black iron ore is carefully separated out by washing. Once the ore is dry, it is put in a furnace over a special mix of charcoal. Before this can be done, however, a special ceremony must be performed. The smith and his assistants pour beer over the furnace and utter ritual prayers to the appropriate spirits. Throughout the day the assistants blow air through bellows onto the coals and adjust the amount of charcoal, raising and lowering the temperature as needed so that the melted sand is reduced over time to iron and slag. The iron and the slag are left to cool overnight. In the morning the smith brings another small quantity of a special beer, and upon arriving at the smithy, he greets the spirits that have overseen the furnace overnight. He sprinkles the beer over and around the furnace and the tools. This is considered a critical part of iron making. If the spirits are not satisfied, the iron will break and the consequences can be disastrous for the warrior or hunter. After the ceremony the pieces of iron are knocked loose from the slag, are reheated, and then are sorted by size so that they can be made into other objects. These pieces are called *mondwa*, and it is these pieces a man buys, not the spear tip or other object. He then asks the smith to make the object specifically for him.

Kenyatta points out that this time-consuming process was not performed often. If old iron was available, such as broken tools, it would be saved and reused. The Kikuyu did not need a great deal of iron; the demand for new iron was likely to come only in years when age-group ceremonies to initiate warriors would take place. In fact, demand was so low in some villages that their smiths never actually made iron. They were able to go through their whole lives using and reusing existing iron.

THE LUO

The Luo's position in Kenya today is an interesting mix of relative power and clear second-class status in comparison to the wealthier and more numerous Kikuyu. The two groups have been bitter rivals for generations, and the rivalry is a major political reality in today's Kenya. As journalist Blaine Harden puts it, "In their contemporary stereotypes of each other, the Luo see the Kikuyu as denatured, money hungry businessmen aping Western values as they betray their African heritage. The Kikuyu see the Luo as histrionic devotees of primitive traditions, with stout hearts, good singing voices and soft heads."[4] In other words, the Kikuyu see the Luo as too old fashioned, and the Luo see the Kikuyu as too modern. Fortunately, the rivalry has not been notoriously bloody, compared, for example, to that between the Hutu and Tutsi in nearby Rwanda.

Many Kenyans still think of themselves as being from the area that their ethnic group inhabits, such as Luoland or Kikuyuland, rather than from the nation of Kenya. This is common in other parts of Africa as well. For many Africans, national borders mean very little. Ethnic groups sometimes find that national borders go right through the middle of their land or that they have been thrown together with other groups with whom they have long-standing hostility. Kenya's borders were drawn by colonists to mark their territorial claims, with little or no regard for the people who already lived there. When Great Britain relinquished Kenya, the newly independent nation maintained the boundaries the British had established, even though these borders made little sense to the Africans who lived there. Luoland is a good example of how the unnatural boundaries of many African nations have made it more difficult to achieve a sense of national identity in the post-independence era. Many Luo actually live in neighboring Uganda, on the other side of Lake Victoria; thus, the political power that their overall numbers might give them is diminished because they are citizens of two different countries. Also, if the border of Kenya had been drawn in a way that separated the Luo and the Kikuyu, the divisiveness that has hindered Kenya might have been avoided.

Between 3 and 4 million Luo live in Kenya, compared to over 5 million Kikuyu. The Luo, despite their fairly wide geographic range and nine separate clans, are one of the most

Fishermen
on Lake Victoria.

cohesive ethnic groups in Kenya. Though it is possible that the Luhya, who live north of Lake Victoria, are more numerous, the Luo are clearly the second most influential group in Kenya today.

The Luo population is centered around the Lake Victoria area in the Nyanza Province. They are excellent fishermen and farmers and are prominent in Kenya as mechanics, machinists, and other skilled tradesmen. Trade unions in Kenya are dominated by Luo. Though it is an oversimplification to say, as some do, that the Kikuyu have the land and the Luo have the skilled labor, this is a common sentiment in Kenya among the other groups, many of whom feel they have been left behind in everything.

Ancestors of the Luo first came to Kenya in around 1000 B.C., but today's Luo are fairly recent arrivals, having pushed their herds south from drought-ridden Sudan in the 1400s, and finally reaching and settling in southern Kenya in the 1700s. Along the way south from Sudan, the Luo mixed with people already established on the lands they passed through. Over time, those who arrived in Lake Victoria established what is now considered the main Luo culture, a result of cultural mixing with the Bantu speakers already in the area.

A cattle disease called rinderpest destroyed their herds in the 1890s and prompted their successful move into fishing and farming. The Luo still graze goats and cattle, but more of them now have farms, not usually larger than thirty-five acres. The rocky, mountainous land creates some problems for farmers, but the Luo have been successful at growing maize, millet, cotton, rice, sugarcane, peanuts, and sweet potatoes. Most farming is done by women now. Men tend to fish or go into trades. There is only a little industry in Luoland, and many Luo live in Nairobi, elsewhere in Kenya, or in neighboring Uganda. The tendency of men to leave home for long periods of time to find employment, and the resulting overburdening of women with both farming and family duties, has created major disruptions in family structure not only among the Luo but also across much of Africa.

WOMEN IN KENYA

Kenya, like the rest of Africa, is a male-dominated society, and many women live in a state of perpetual exhaustion. It is estimated that women do as much as 80 percent of the work in rural communities, in addition to their chores in the home and as mothers. Women do most of the planting, weeding, and harvesting of crops. In communities without running water, it is usually the women and children who are responsible for retrieving water and transporting it home in heavy jugs, sometimes for miles. Women take food to market and sell or trade it and do heavy chores around the home, including patching the walls and repairing the roof.

Sometimes this is necessary because the men are not there. Many men have had to leave home to get jobs that pay wages in cities. Most of Kenya's women do not work for wages. However, this association of women with nonpaying work and men with wages has resulted in a situation in which men control the money in families. As a result, a man who still lives at home may not feel that he owes all of his wages to his family.

Because Kenyan women are looked down upon as second-class citizens, Kenya has been unable to establish a good record of legal rights for women. Women have trouble buying and inheriting land. Wife beating commonly goes unpunished, and many women have no access to birth control. The cruel practice of clitoridectomy, or female circumcision, leaves many Kenyan women's genitals maimed, painful, and subject to infection for life.

This situation is slowly changing. Girls now have an equal opportunity to attend school. Kisumu has had a woman mayor, and several women have been elected to Parliament. Organizations such as the National Woman's Council of Kenya lobby Parliament, teach women skills needed for wage employment, and give women small business loans. Life is still difficult for women in Kenya, but it is improving.

Kisumu, the main city in Luoland, is located on Lake Victoria, which is called Lolwe in Jaluo (or Dhaluo), the local language. (Different spellings of words in African languages is common because writing the language down has often only been done recently, and spellings are put down the way the words sound. There is less of an emphasis on "correctness" than there is in English.) Kisumu is the third largest city in Kenya, but it has been in decline since boat travel across the lake was replaced by roads and the railway as the main conduit for trade between East Africa and the interior.

The Luo as a whole tend to be culturally independent, despite their long history of intermingling. For example, the Luo are the only group in Kenya who do not practice circumcision, and they are one of the few groups in this part of Africa who traditionally had a powerful king (called a *ruoth*) as their head. A person became the *ruoth* not because of family connections but because of character and demonstrated leadership. The *ruoth* made decisions for the clan in consultation with a Council of Elders. In most other ethnic groups in Kenya (at least before the colonial period), the Council of Elders was the only community authority, and age groups had great importance.

Young Luo school children. When a high-school diploma is received, it is a symbol of the end of childhood.

Tribal practices are less closely followed today than in the past, but the Luo still have strong ties to their ancient customs. Some older Luo can still be recognized by a gap of six lower front teeth, knocked out as a rite of passage into adulthood, but younger Luo tend to see a high-school diploma as an altogether better symbol of the end of childhood. The majority of Luo are now Christian, but like elsewhere in Christian-influenced Africa, their customs are really a blend of Christianity and ancient beliefs. Jaluo is less commonly spoken today, but many Luo still speak it in addition to kiSwahili and English.

THE MAASAI

In Kenya today it might be difficult to tell a Luo from a Kikuyu. The chances are, however, that even the casual observer would be able to pick out a Maasai. The Maasai are perhaps the most famous ethnic group in Kenya and Tanzania, although their numbers are actually quite small, probably somewhere around 250,000 total. The Maasai cut impressive figures on their ancestral lands, and many of them have remained traditional in their dress and customs. The Maasai (sometimes spelled Masai) are the warriors of the savanna. They have a deserved reputation for their athleticism and their skill as hunters. Traditionally, the Maasai could run down prey and kill it with spears. Because of the great danger of this technique, they have maintained a reputation for courage and ferocity as hunters and warriors. Now, many Maasai are better known for the shows they put on for tourists, which display a traditional dance style of jumping ramrod straight up into the air. Their tall thin frames, dressed in reds and golds, jet upward against a blue sky and the backdrop of the savanna while tourists snap pictures—for a steep price. Women adorned with dozens of stiff disc-shaped bead necklaces also dance and sing while children hawk souvenirs.

The Maasai are proud of their culture—to the point of snobbery, some outsiders think. A common derisive term the Maasai use for Europeans is *ilori-daa-enjekat*, which means "those who conceal their farts." The Maasai, who still live almost entirely off herding and hunting, were traditionally so scornful of agriculturalists that they would not dig into the ground even to bury their own dead. They feel, or at least

A Maasai man pre-pares another's hair for participation in a marriage ceremony.

used to feel, that all cattle in the world belong by divine right to them, and they are taking back what is rightfully theirs when they steal cattle from others.

The Maasai lifestyle centers around cattle. They have dozens of names for the different color patterns on their cattle, and one of the skills boys are expected to master is to recognize each animal by appearance and to tell if any are missing by this manner rather than by counting. The Maasai live primarily in the southern end of the Great Rift Valley and on the nearby game reserves in settlements called *bomas,* which consist of circles of twig huts surrounded by berms high enough to keep cattle in. They rarely slaughter their cattle but still use them as their main food source by a technique that allows them to tap the animal's blood without harming it. They then drink the blood mixed with curdled milk. During the dry season, the Maasai leave their *bomas* for months at a time to follow their herds deeper into the Rift Valley in search of pastureland and water.

The Maasai are organized around age groups. In such societies, everyone born within a set period of time, usually a couple of years, is linked for life. Within a year or so of turning

Maasai boys learn to recognize cattle in their herds by appearance.

age fifteen, Maasai boys go through a group ritual to become *morani*, or warriors. They are circumcised (to show no sign of pain is a way to demonstrate courage), after which they are covered with a red ochre and go off together to spend time with their elders learning survival techniques and other customs of the Maasai. In the past, part of becoming a *moran* was to bring down a lion by oneself, using only a spear. Often the time in the brush with their elders was the only formal education *morani* were considered to need. Now they are required to go to school, the time in the brush has been curtailed, and it is forbidden by Kenyan law to hunt lions.

That does not mean that outlawed practices are dead, though; the Maasai are notoriously reluctant to accept outside authority. In recent times they have coexisted uneasily with the modern government of Kenya. Many of their traditions are outlawed because they are at odds with efforts to preserve and rebuild the dwindling numbers of large animals on the savanna, which are the backbone of the tourist economy. Efforts to get the Maasai to "settle down" have been strongly rebuffed, and they still do not seem to have a clear understanding of the concept of ownership, especially individual ownership of land.

Age groups remain an essential part of Maasai identity throughout life, particularly for males. When the *morani* grow older, they retire as a group and become village elders. Village elders are the governing body of each Maasai community, and they make decisions through discussion and consensus. Societies that function without a ruler and are organized around small communities are called stateless societies, and the Maasai, and most of the ethnic groups in Kenya other than the Luo, are good examples of these.

The Maasai language is called Maa and is Nilotic in origin, meaning that it is derived from the peoples of the Nile basin in modern Sudan. This accounts for the Maasai's pastoralist, or livestock-raising, culture—the Nilotic groups came down into Kenya originally behind their flocks. Despite their linguistic connection to the Luo, it is with the Kikuyu and other Bantu groups that they have forged closer links. The Kikuyu and Maasai are particularly intertwined, especially by marriage. In the past, women who married into the other group often functioned as informal ambassadors during times of hostility, and they had a special status for this reason.

OTHER ETHNIC GROUPS

The majority of Kenyans are not Maasai, Luo, or Kikuyu. They belong to one of the approximately forty other ethnic groups in modern Kenya. A few of the more prominent of these groups are the Luhya, a large group in the west; the Turkana, a nomadic group centered around Lake Turkana on the northern border; the Somalis in the northeast; and the Kalenjin, a collection of small groups in southern Kenya. The Turkana, Luhya, Somalis, Kalenjin, and other groups, including the Swahili culture along the coast, are proud of their distinct cultures and histories.

Many Kenyans continue to dress in traditional ethnic styles, pay deference to traditional spirits, eat traditional foods, and otherwise continue to identify with their ethnic group as

INDIANS IN KENYA

In Kenya, Indians are considered Asians. They played an indirect role in East Africa for hundreds of years. In the Arab trading era, India was one of the ports regularly visited. Indian products and crops soon found their way to East African shores, although Indian people themselves did not. India was called "the Jewel in the Crown" of the British colonial empire, and many Indians came to other British protectorates in the early twentieth century, primarily as laborers. Thousands of Indians came to Kenya to help build the Mombasa-Uganda railroad. When it was completed, some Indians stayed on, primarily as merchants because they were not permitted to own land. They were perceived as "colored" by the European colonists, and though they were not treated as poorly as the Africans were, they were clearly on the wrong side of the color line.

Despite their inferior status compared to whites, Indians fared well economically compared to African Kenyans, and thus became targets of resentment by the Africans. After independence, many Indians felt that there would be vengeance against them in African-ruled Kenya, so they began to leave in large numbers. Half of the Asian population left Kenya in the first decade after independence. Along the Islamic coast, particularly in Mombasa as well as in Nairobi, there is still a substantial Indian presence, as reflected by the popularity of Indian music, restaurants, and movies.

A tribal dancer in a full ceremonial costume of bones and feathers.

much as or more than they identify with being Kenyan. This brings a cultural richness to Kenya, but it has also been a drawback to Kenya's development as a nation. Governing the country is more difficult because groups often oppose or mistrust each other for no reason beyond long-standing dislike. Likewise, it is clear that those in power see it as part of their job to make sure their own ethnic groups benefit from government funds and projects more than others do. Many Kenyans, particularly the better-educated ones, see continuing tribalism as one of the biggest obstacles Kenya will need to overcome to fulfill its potential as a modern nation.

From Fossils
to Foreigners

Every year anthropologists discover new fossils that help us to understand how humans evolved. Fossil evidence suggests that the earliest human ancestors evolved in and around modern Kenya as long as 3 million years ago. For this reason, Kenya today is still one of the world's primary sites for archaeological research.

By studying similarities and differences in culture and language among current ethnic groups in Kenya, as well as cave paintings, pottery, and jewelry found at sites of early human communities, archaeologists and linguists have proposed a number of different theories explaining how each of Kenya's broad ethnic groups came to be where they are today. Most agree that, with only a few exceptions, the current groups were in Kenya by A.D. 1500. For the two millennia from 500 B.C. to A.D. 1500, the picture is less clear, but scholars agree that most of the approximately forty ethnic groups of modern Kenya evolved from only four original language groups: Bantu, Nilotic, Cushitic, and Somali. Cushitic-language speakers are named for the ancient kingdom of Cush (now Ethiopia), and both they and the Somali-language speakers still tend to live close to the borders of those two countries. Because these two groups have relatively few members and are isolated in northern Kenya, they do not play as large a role in Kenyan history or in present-day Kenya as do the other two groups, the Bantu speakers and the Nilotic speakers.

These two language groups have ancient, complex, and only partially understood histories. In essence, the Nilotic speakers are descendants of a group that pushed south from the Nile Delta in North Africa centuries ago either because of drought, their nomadic lifestyle, or both. The Bantu came eastward from West Africa in roughly the same period. Nilotic and Bantu languages are as different from each other as, for example, Russian and Spanish, but often Bantu-language

Primitive art provides evidence of early human ancestry in and around Kenya.

speakers can understand at least some of what different Bantu-language speakers are saying, and the same is true for the Nilotic languages.

BANTU SPEAKERS

The most important of these groups is the Bantu speakers. *Bantu* is not the name of a tribe or even of a specific language. It is the general term used for a group of people spread over wide regions of Africa whose language evolved from a common root language, proto-Bantu, and whose cultures have certain elements in common. The Kikuyu are modern-day descendants of these early Bantu speakers.

The Bantu speakers' two biggest cultural advantages were their ability to make iron tools and their knowledge of how to cultivate crops. Even though the era starting between the second and fifth centuries A.D. is called the Iron Age, agriculture was the far more important of these two developments. Once methods of agriculture were developed, larger areas of land could be populated. It was no longer necessary for the Bantu speakers and others to stay in or near jungles or other areas where they could count on being able to hunt or gather enough food; now they could live wherever conditions permitted them to grow crops. This is how parts of Kenya first came to be settled by Bantu-speaking people, probably between the years 300 and 900.

NILOTIC SPEAKERS

Bantu speakers were not the only group moving into Kenya. From the north, Nilotic people were also moving down into Kenya. The Luo are descendants of these early Nilotic-language speakers.

Nilotic people were pastoralists, people whose central activity is tending herds of livestock. Pastoralists tend to be nomadic, and thus the boundaries of their ethnic groups are always in flux. Pastoralists are usually contrasted with agriculturalists, who grow crops and thus tend to stay in one area and build permanent communities. Often pastoralists and agriculturalists are able to coexist peacefully. Over time, however, agricultural communities tend to supplant pastoral ones not only because agriculture can support larger numbers of people than herding but also because when groups intermarry, the tendency is for their descendants to choose the more settled lifestyle. Since the Bantu were agriculturalists, this partly accounts for why they, rather than the Nilotic peoples, became the dominant ethnic stock in most of Kenya.

EARLY COASTAL HISTORY

In the same period of time that the Bantu and other groups were settling in the savannas, highlands, and deserts of Kenya, the outside world was "discovering" the coast. Because early visitors such as the Greeks, Persians, Ethiopians, and Arabs were already writing down histories and travel narratives, detailed descriptions of their contacts with coastal Kenya exist as far back as 500 B.C. Others, including Indian and Chinese traders, also explored the Kenya coast in the course of trading voyages.

Initially seafaring nations were only interested in establishing trade with the region, none wanted to colonize the area. Wind patterns along the east coast of Africa are such that, at the time, small sailing ships had only a short period each year that the prevailing winds permitted them to make their trade runs. African communities along the coast from Somalia to Tanzania, most notably Mombasa and Lamu in present-day Kenya, grew in response to their new status as

Arab sailors came in contact with coastal Kenyans as early as 500 B.C.

ports. During the rest of the year, when the ships were unable to come to Kenya, merchants and traders from Mombasa and Lamu would travel inland and to smaller communities along the coast, bringing with them foreign goods for trade and leaving with items for export. Thus, during the short window of time when foreign traders were in port, goods were already centralized in the port towns. In this way, the ethnic groups of Kenya were able to get items such as beads and cotton and some iron tools from the foreigners, in exchange for ivory, rhinoceros horn, tortoise shell, and coconut oil. In later years, the cargo leaving Africa's eastern ports would also include large numbers of slaves.

THE SWAHILI CULTURE

Only one of the early trading groups had a lasting influence on the coastal area, then known as Azania and later called the Land of Zenj. Some Arabs settled permanently and began intermarrying. The area soon became Islamic and began developing its own unique culture, Swahili, a blend of Arabic and native African influences. Notable evidence of this blending is the language kiSwahili, a Bantu language with many Arabic borrowings. Today coastal towns such as the small island of Lamu still look like something out of an Arabian Nights novel, with minarets, domed buildings, and open-air bazaars, or *souks*.

By the fourteenth century the term *Swahili* referred to an Islamic society because of its religion and many aspects of its culture, but it also referred to an African society because of its language and people. However, many books on African history tend to overestimate the role of the Arabs in the creation of coastal African culture in Kenya and surrounding areas. According to historian Kevin Shillington,

> This is not to deny the extremely important contribution of Islamic Arab immigrants to the further development of Swahili culture and trading networks. But what previously tended to be overlooked was the extent of the indigenous African input to the early development of coastal trade and the spread of Swahili culture and society.[5]

Until recently most histories of Africa were written by non-Africans, and this influenced the way in which Africa

Intermarriage between Kenyans and Arabs led to a blending of customs and the development of the Swahili culture.

was portrayed. Just as histories of the United States often downplay the level of sophistication of the Native Americans, non-African historians writing about Africa often saw fit to imply that culture and civilization arrived only from the outside. A good example of this general assumption is the widely held belief that Arabs introduced the coastal Africans to the idea of long-distance trade. In fact, trade had been in place for some time, and coastal towns were already well established. The Arabs' contribution was to link East Africans to world markets, not to make a fundamental change in their culture. Evidence of trade expeditions to inland regions of Kenya dates back to the fifth century A.D., long before the arrival of "outsiders," with salt being the main product going inland and copper and ivory the main products going to the coast.

Over several centuries a unique blend of African and Arabic cultures continued to evolve along the Kenya coast. Because the Arabs had a written language and a literary culture, it is from this period that we begin to have good historical records for Africa. In Kenya, as in many other parts of Africa, oral tradition had been an effective means of handing down history and culture. It was the job of the oral historian to remember all the history of his community and recite it at important gatherings. Most oral histories go back in great detail, around five hundred years. This is an astonishing feat of memory, whose accuracy is well corroborated by other sources, but oral recitations of history do not reach as far back as the early written records in Swahili.

Early historians included al-Masudi in the tenth century and Ibn Battutah in the fourteenth century. From these records, modern historians have determined that the Land of Zenj comprised city-states. Arabs, including a ruling sultan, were at the top socially and politically. The majority of the townspeople were kiSwahili-speaking African Muslims. They worked at trades and professions, such as ship captain and craftsman. The lowest class was made up of non-Muslims, who were often slaves taken from inland. They did heavy labor on farms and manual labor making cotton cloth, beads, and other items for use locally or for export.

THE PORTUGUESE

In 1498 a new chapter of Kenyan history began when Vasco da Gama sailed around the Cape of Good Hope and up the East African coast. He saw well-established city-states and evidence of great riches. He also saw a new source of trade for Portugal, one that could be reached without going through the Mediterranean, where piracy was rampant. The Portuguese decided to claim the coastal area of Kenya for themselves and came into ports such as Mombasa with heavily armed ships. They demanded that the ruling sultan become a Portuguese subject and show evidence of his loyalty in the form of expensive gifts and promises to cease trade with Arabs and Persians. The Portuguese claimed that this was a holy war against non-Christian infidels. Although some sultans gave in, such as those in Lamu and Malindi, the sultan of Mombasa did not. He kept trading with Muslims, and Mombasa was sacked for a second time in 1505 and then again in 1528 and 1529. In 1599 the Portuguese completed a fortress in Mombasa named Fort Jesus, which became the main center of Portuguese power for the next century. The Portuguese never actually settled in large numbers, and as Portuguese power declined globally, they eventually were pushed out of East Africa by the native Swahili population.

SLAVERY

By the 1600s the east coast of Kenya was well known for world trade. It was also a major source of slaves. Most of the slaves that were brought to North America came from West Africa because the distance was so much shorter, and thus the routes were more profitable for the slavers. Plantations in other parts of the world wanted slaves too, however, and for them the East African coast was a good source. The French

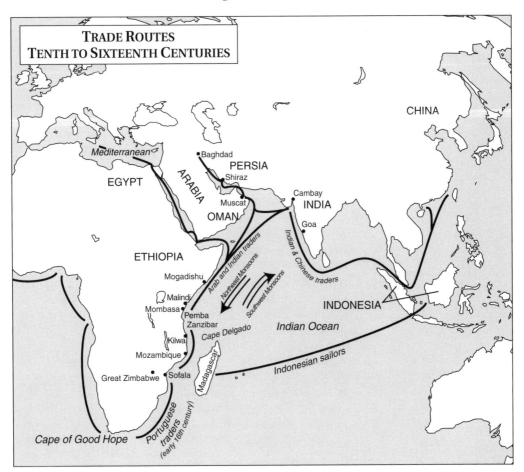

TRADE ROUTES
TENTH TO SIXTEENTH CENTURIES

THE SACK OF MOMBASA

In 1505 João de Barros and Hans Mayr, sailors on a Portuguese ship, were eyewitnesses to the Portuguese sack of Mombasa. The following account is adapted from their memoirs, portions of which appear in Kevin Shillington's *History of Africa*.

The Moors of Mombasa had built a strongpoint with many guns at the entrance of the harbour, which is very narrow. When we entered, the first ship was fired on by the Moors from both sides. We promptly replied to the fire, and with such intensity that their gunpowder in their strongpoint caught fire.

After the Moors fled, the Portuguese fleet entered the harbor and prepared to burn the town.

But when they went to burn the town they were received by the Moors with a shower of arrows and stones. The town has more than 600 houses which are thatched with palm leaves which are collected green for this purpose. In between the stone dwelling-houses there are wooden houses with porches and stables for cattle. . . . Once the fire started it raged all night long, and many houses collapsed and a large quantity of goods were destroyed.

The next morning the Portuguese went ashore. The few people who remained in the burned-out buildings threw stones at them. In the skirmish that followed, four Portuguese were killed.

The Grand-Captain went straight to the royal palace . . . and hoisted our flag, shouting: Portugal, Portugal. The death of these four was avenged by that of 1513 Moors. . . . The Grand-Captain ordered that the town should be sacked, and that each man should carry off to his ship whatever he found: so that at the end there would be a division of the spoil, each man to receive a twentieth of what he found. The same rule was made for gold, silver and pearls. Then everyone started to plunder the town and to search the houses, forcing open the doors with axes and iron bars. There was a large quantity of cotton cloth . . . in the town, for the whole coast gets its cotton cloth from here. So the Grand-Captain got a good share . . . for himself. A large quantity of rich silk and gold embroidered clothes was seized, and carpets also; one . . . without equal for beauty, was sent to the King of Portugal, together with many other valuables.

A slave market in Zanzibar.

needed slaves for their sugar plantations located on islands in the Indian Ocean. Brazilian slave ships could sail south around the Cape of Good Hope to pick up their human cargo, thus avoiding the antislavery ships that were disrupting trade in the North Atlantic. Slaves were already part of the Swahili culture along the coast; those slaves who were not needed by the Swahili were sold, in the tens of thousands annually, at markets such as the one on the island of Zanzibar south of Kenya. Many more slaves were sent to Arabia and Persia.

THE MAASAI CIVIL WARS

In the seventeenth century a new group of Nilotic herders moved south into Kenya. This group, the Maasai, would have far reaching effects on the groups already established there. It was common for the nomadic Maasai to spend much of the year covering great distances in search of pasture for their cattle. Over the years this continual battle to feed and expand their herds (and thus survive themselves) produced an aggressive culture, able to move quickly and willing to fight anyone who resisted them. The Maasai were able to sweep into and through the Great Rift Valley all the way down into Tanzania and establish themselves as the main cultural group in those areas.

Despite periodic raids against groups such as the Kikuyu and Kalenjin, especially when drought or epidemics of rinderpest destroyed Maasai herds, the Maasai were able to

FORT JESUS

Because of repeated skirmishes in the Mombasa area between rival African groups, the Portuguese decided sometime around 1590 to build a fort in Mombasa to protect themselves. More importantly, they wanted to ensure that, regardless of which local group controlled the city at any given time, the Portuguese could continue to be able to use the excellent natural harbor as a base of trade. According to Richard Trillo, author of *Kenya: The Rough Guide,* "Once completed, the fort became the focus of everything that mattered in Mombasa." The Portuguese, however, would soon find that the fort did not for long serve the purposes they had intended. In 1631 every last Portuguese was killed when local people took over the fort. Though the Portuguese eventually reclaimed the fort, over the next approximately two hundred years the fort would change hands eight more times.

Today visitors to Mombasa can tour Fort Jesus, which has been preserved as a monument and museum. Many visitors comment on how much the fort resembles a classic European castle of its era with its high, angled walls constructed so that anyone trying to scale the sides could be picked off by crossfire. Inside are quiet, shady courtyards and dwellings that once housed soldiers. In one of the fort's rooms, graffiti can still be seen that was drawn by Portuguese sentries to while away their long shifts.

coexist with other groups in the area. This is partly because the Maasai were open to the cultural practices of other groups, such as circumcision and age-group initiations. They also had no objections to intermarriage with the Kikuyu, the Kalenjin, and others. Over time this created a sense of mutual understanding and commonality. In fact, most Maasai aggression was directed against other Maasai. Because of their nomadic lifestyle, the Maasai tended to see themselves as members of their own small band rather than as part of a larger ethnic group. Hostility toward other Maasai bands was inevitable because they all were competing for the same thing—cattle and grazing land.

In the second half of the nineteenth century, life for everyone in the Rift Valley area was impacted by what have been called the Maasai civil wars. By this time trade routes were well established between the coast and the Rift Valley area, and the Maasai's nearly continual raiding of each other and of trade parties made venturing into the Great Rift Valley frightening. Missionaries, slavers, and traders alike were attacked by the Maasai. Trade and missionary work still went on, however. Although the Maasai might have been able to drive foreigners completely out of the area, they were more interested in raiding them. In the years to come, many Maasai would regret that they had not done more to remove this threat to their way of life.

Most newcomers to Kenya in the nineteenth century and earlier were in one way or another looking to profit from its land and people. One group stands out as having a different goal.

CHRISTIAN MISSIONARIES

In the mid–nineteenth century, Mombasa was considered a good point from which to launch missionary efforts to convert Africans to Christianity. Missionaries and explorers often traveled together because the interior of the continent was virtually unknown. However, while the explorers saw themselves as only temporarily in Kenya looking for information about geography and natural resources, their traveling companions were looking for a good place to settle and go about the business of building churches and preaching Christianity.

The earliest Christian missionary was Johann Krapf, who arrived in Nyali in the Mombasa area in 1844. Within two months the German missionary had lost both his wife and

Covering great distances in order to feed their herds, the Maasai became the main cultural group in the Rift Valley and Tanzania.

his baby daughter to malaria. Undaunted, Krapf pushed a few miles inland and established the first Christian mission in East Africa. From this base near Mombasa, Krapf spent the rest of his life doing the necessary groundwork for future missionaries, including deciphering Swahili grammar so that missionaries could learn the language and translating the Bible into Swahili. He also explored Kenya extensively. In fact, the name *Kenya* comes from Krapf's misunderstanding of *Kere-Ngayah*, the Kikuyu word for Mount Kenya. He began calling the area by this name, and over time the label stuck.

The African missionaries' lives were very hard. Not only were they isolated, often for life, from everything that was familiar, but they were also rarely, if ever, welcomed as newcomers. Kenyan ethnic groups as a whole were hostile toward missionaries because it was quite clear that the missionaries' goal was to undercut or destroy traditional beliefs and customs. Though the missionaries believed they were helping Africans, most African ethnic groups did not think they needed the help. Their religious beliefs and practices made sense to them and had long histories that tied them together as a people. If it were not for the fact that westerners did bring some improvements to their lives, such as tools and medicines, it is unlikely that the missionaries would have been as successful as they eventually were. Today slightly more than half of all Kenyans are Christians.

Western missionaries brought tools and medicine as well as religion to Kenya.

THE MUUNGANO NATIONAL CHOIR AND THE *MISSA LUBA*

The importance of Christianity to Kenya, as well as the particular stamp that African Kenyans have put on the faith, is evident in the *Missa Luba*. This is the African version of the Roman Catholic mass, which was made internationally famous by the Muungano National Choir of Kenya.

The mass is performed by singers clothed in traditional costumes. Accompaniment is on traditional drums and gourds. The words are sung in Latin, the traditional language of the Catholic service, but the rhythms and harmonies are distinctly African. For example, many sections are organized around call-and-response, whereby a line from one singer is answered by a chorus. The mass is actually Congolese in origin, but it has become associated with Kenya because the choir director, Bonifacio Mganga, and the members of the choir are Kenyans.

The mass consists of the five pieces most closely associated with the Catholic mass. The best-known piece in the *Missa Luba* is the "Sanctus" ("Holy, Holy, Holy Lord God of Hosts"). This piece was used in the movie *If*, which was actor Malcolm McDowell's first starring role, to illustrate his feelings of outsider status as a boarding school student and his longing for a more exotic, exciting life.

Although Christian missionaries have been criticized for disrespecting indigenous religions, it is obvious while watching the Muungano National Choir, that, however Christianity came to Kenya, many modern Kenyans feel strongly about a faith that is now clearly their own.

In addition to being sincere and voluntarily subjecting themselves to many hardships to spread the "true" word of God, the precolonial Christian missionaries were preaching Protestant morals, values, and practices. For example, they insisted that baptized Africans take "Christian" names, such as Alice or Samuel, without apparently realizing that their idea of a Christian name was at best an English translation rather than a strictly biblical name. Nonetheless, many Kenyans embraced Christianity because, at its core, it was not really inconsistent with their traditional ideas, such as the existence of a supreme being, a powerful being (Jesus) with mixed attributes of a god and a human, and the continued existence of the dead in another realm. Even today Kenyan Christianity is distinctly African, mixing ancient African beliefs with Christian ones.

Though many Africans were converted in the last half of the nineteenth or early in the twentieth centuries, these conversions came at a high price to the missionaries. Many died of diseases such as sleeping sickness, which is caused by the bite of the tsetse fly. Some missionaries were killed by the Maasai or others. To a certain extent, the missionaries unfairly bore the brunt of the hostility directed toward other early white intruders, who often took what they wanted by force and violence. Because the missionaries looked the same as these other whites and were settling at approximately the same time, these peaceable, unarmed evangelists became easy targets.

THE SOURCE OF THE NILE

At the turn of the twentieth century, most African Kenyans had never seen a white face. For those who had, the likelihood is that it was the face of an early explorer. Many of these early explorers were on geographical missions. Since there were no airplanes or motor vehicles, the only way to discover what lay in the interior of Africa was to travel there by foot. Expeditions often took years. Once explorers disappeared into the savannas, rain forests, or deserts, their whereabouts and fate were unknown since there were no telephones or other means of communicating with the outside world. Early explorers died from diseases or wounds more often than from attacks by residents of the areas they explored. Because they were simply passing through, they were generally not perceived as threats to traditional ways. Thus, where missionaries might have had difficulty getting help from local groups, explorers were able to trade goods they had brought with them in exchange for local scouts, supplies, and other necessities.

One of the goals of early East African explorers such as Richard Burton was to find the source of the Nile River. The interior of Africa was largely unknown, but the assumption was that the source of the Nile must lie deep in the heart of the continent. Some explorers speculated that it might lie as far south as Kenya, many miles inland from the coast. The Nile is the longest river in the world, and the Nile Delta, which passes through the Sahara Desert and eventually spills into the Mediterranean, has been an important trading and agricultural center since the time of the Egyptian pharaohs. The British had established friendly trade relations with Egypt by the mid-nineteenth century and were interested in expanding their dominance in the area. However, it was clear that without the existence of a free-flowing Nile River, Egypt would be nothing but desert. Great Britain began to fear that it might be possible to dam the Nile at its source, but at that time no one knew the source of the mighty river. British expeditions were launched to find the source and lay claim to the territory surrounding it.

Explorer Richard Burton sought the source of the Nile River.

Originally their interest was not in this territory itself, but just in keeping another rival power such as Germany from ruining Egypt by damming the Nile. Eventually the source of the Nile was determined to be Lake Victoria, and though the idea of damming the Nile at its source had come to seem preposterous, the side effect of all the exploration was that the tropical interior of Kenya was now familiar to the British. Once they had seen it, they decided they wanted it for themselves.

Despite forays by a few missionaries and explorers, inland Kenya continued free of outside influence in this early period of European interest. This was to change in the mid-1800s, when Europe turned its attention once more to the vast riches of Africa.

4

FROM COLONY TO INDEPENDENT NATION

Before the end of the nineteenth century, almost no foreign countries had claims on African land. Over hundreds of years the Arabs, the only group who had stayed for long in Africa, had become thoroughly blended with indigenous Africans into the Swahili culture. The only outsiders any ethnic group had to worry about were other African groups encroaching onto its land or interfering with trade. As the nineteenth century drew to a close, however, the major European powers were meeting in Berlin; the outcome of that meeting would forever change Kenya and the rest of Africa.

THE SCRAMBLE FOR AFRICA

The Berlin Conference of 1884 started with two goals. In the Congo basin of western Africa, King Leopold of Belgium had established a colony and had begun exporting rubber and other goods down the Congo River. Although he saw the Congo as a personal possession, he had invested a great deal of his nation's money in developing this export business. He did not want to see any other foreign power moving into the Congo basin and setting up similar operations. The Berlin Conference established that Leopold had, to the European mind at least, "legitimate authority" in the Congo, and thus the region was off-limits to others.

The participants in the conference also agreed that any claim by a European power to another part of Africa would be considered valid only if that power had "effectively occupied" the area. This treaty language was designed to distinguish a European country that was simply the main trading power in a part of Africa from one that had an exclusive claim to that area. This was primarily meant to preclude the British from claiming that their "spheres of influence" over much of North Africa gave them a right to call the land around these centers theirs, as Leopold had succeeded in doing in the Congo.

The Berlin Conference could have worked to keep the African continent out of European hands and to maintain its status as an independent trading partner, but that was never the conference participants' intent. Instead, the European powers quickly began moving onto African soil to set up colonies, which would enable them to claim the land as their own. Germany immediately declared a protectorate in what today is Tanzania, just south of Kenya, based on a few rather suspect treaties a German agent had negotiated with some local African leaders.

European powers wanted Africa for a number of reasons. Competition among themselves made them wish for a broader base of power, a wider market for their goods, and a new source of natural resources for their own use. Based on what they had seen in the coastal ports, and from reports of missionaries and early explorers, they knew that Africa had vast untapped resources. Their general attitude was similar to that of the United States towards the Native Americans: Anything the indigenous people of an area did not seem to be using was free for the taking since they could not be said to own anything that they did not appear to value.

THE BRITISH CLAIM IN EAST AFRICA

The British had particularly strong interests in laying claim to eastern Africa. They had already established spheres of influence in North Africa, particularly along the Nile Delta in Sudan and Egypt. The Nile flows from its source, Lake Victoria, and crosses the Sahara Desert on its way to the Mediterranean. Recognizing that the free flow of the Nile was essential to life along the delta, the British had begun to worry that the Nile might be dammed by an unfriendly European power such as Germany.

When Germany laid claim to land in East Africa, it became clear to the British that they would need to do the same if they wished to maintain their power in northern Africa. In 1890 a separate treaty between Germany and Great Britain confirmed that the region of Uganda and eastward to the coast was to be controlled by the British. The British government immediately chartered a private business venture, the British East Africa Corporation, to begin establishing inland forts, which it could call colonies, and thus lock in its claims to the surrounding land. In 1895 the British government took

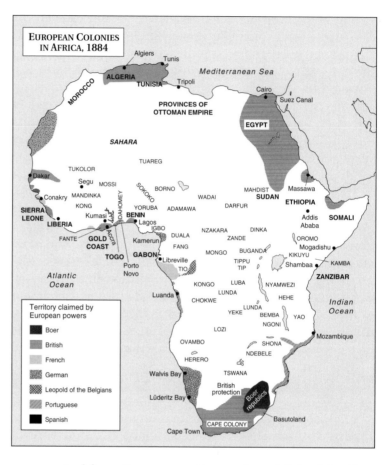

EUROPEAN COLONIES
IN AFRICA, 1884

over control from the corporation and established the East
African Protectorate in what is now roughly present-day
Kenya, Uganda, southern Somalia, and Zanzibar.

Initially the British considered Kenya an inconvenient
barrier that they would have to cross to get from the coast to
what interested them—the source of the Nile, which they
had determined to be Lake Victoria, and the fertile lands of
Uganda, just west of the lake. The border between Uganda
and Kenya was originally the Great Rift Valley. To establish a
protectorate in the area, the British had agreed to the stipu-
lation that any permanent settlements would be in Kenya
rather than in Uganda. When they saw the Kenya highlands
and the areas immediately west of the border, they promptly
moved the border between Kenya and Uganda from the Rift
Valley to Lake Victoria, thus making the highlands open to
future settlement.

THE MOMBASA-UGANDA RAILROAD

At the turn of the twentieth century, few British citizens were interested in relocating to Kenya, a place that must have seemed almost as far away as the moon. In 1900 only 480 Europeans lived within the boundaries of Kenya. When the British began building a railroad between Mombasa and Lake Victoria, it was primarily to facilitate trade with Uganda, not settlement in the inland parts of Kenya. Most of the British saw the railroad as a foolish business proposition, and it quickly gained the nickname "the Lunatic Express." It would be prohibitively expensive, they thought, for the amount of commerce it would generate. In fact, the corporation that built the railroad was secretly beginning to agree with this analysis; it thought that the only way to avoid financial ruin was to bring in a large group of people who would use the railroad. These people would not be Africans, however—the railroad had not been built to transport them. British settlers would need to be enticed to come to Kenya as farmers. The railroad would then be the way their products could be brought to market, and it would serve as their link to the outside world.

The Mombasa-Uganda Railroad was originally built to facilitate trade.

At frequent intervals along the route, depots were built. One such depot was located on the Ngongo Bargas plain, where the Maasai and Kikuyu traditionally met to trade. This depot became the center of trade for the entire region and evolved into today's capital city of Nairobi.

Although two important chiefs, Lenana of the Maasai and Waiyaki of the Kikuyu, got along well with the British and saw advantages in their presence, their opinion was not shared by many others, including many Kikuyu and the Nandi. The Nandi lived in the Great Rift Valley and fought fiercely against the British until they were forcibly subdued in 1905. All initial resistance to British expansion inland had been put down by force before 1910. Africans had guns, but they were older models, and they were not allowed to buy the new breech-loading repeater rifles used by the British. Also, the British had Maxims, the first machine guns. Hilaire Belloc, a writer opposed to British colonialism, penned the following lines about the certain outcome of British force against the Africans: "Whatever happens, we have got/The Maxim gun, and they have not."[6]

SQUATTERS ON THEIR OWN LAND

Most of the Africans building the railroad were not there by choice. They were forced to work laying tracks across their own land. More ominous, however, was their widespread loss of the most fertile land in Kenya. When Great Britain moved the boundary between Uganda and Kenya, it set aside the highlands for white settlement. Suddenly Africans were squatters on their own land, and the British kept coming. In the first fifteen years of the new century, over five thousand Britons settled in the highlands, three thousand of whom had large estates. The Kikuyu were particularly hurt by this because they were the main group in the highlands.

The Africans were forced into reserves, much as the Native Americans had been during the westward expansion of the United States. These reserves were usually in the least arable regions, and as the numbers of whites grew, the British felt free to encroach on these lands and push more and more Kikuyu and others onto smaller patches of land. In fact, after World War I the British government gave away land nearly free to returning soldiers as an incentive to move to Kenya to increase the white presence there.

The Kikuyu saw that only a small portion of the land they had been forced from was actually being cultivated, and they were forced to subsist on what they could grow in the less fertile areas. Likewise, they were not permitted to grow profitable export crops such as coffee; this was reserved for British farmers. It was clear that the settlers were not as effective as the Kikuyu and others had been at growing local crops. Many colonists had never farmed before—and certainly not tropical crops—so cash subsidies and, of course, cheap African labor were needed to keep many farmers solvent. During the same time, Ugandan exports grew, evidence that it was the switch from native to white land management that produced the decline.

BRITISH REPRESSION

Resentment grew among Africans, fanned by repressive laws designed to create an Eden for the British at African expense. Many, although not all, settlers wanted Kenya to evolve into another Australia, where indigenous people had been completely pushed to the side in favor of the whites. Whites wanted the Kenya Colony, as it was now called, to be a white society that was served by Africans. To make that happen, they enforced a strict "color line." Particularly loathsome to the native Africans were new taxes and a pass system, called *kipande*, which restricted movements of Africans on their own ancestral lands. Passes could only be obtained by those Africans who were employed off the reserve; otherwise, people were not permitted to leave. Employers could write comments about a person on his or her pass. A bad comment might mean harassment by police or potential difficulty when looking for new employment. Asians were also subjected to restrictions on their activities because, as elsewhere in British colonies, they were considered "colored."

British-imposed taxes had a particularly devastating effect on native Africans. Most East Africans were subsistence farmers who bartered small surpluses for those items they could not grow or make for themselves. They had no need for money. The British established an annual "hut tax," which required all adult males to pay an amount equivalent to one month's full-time wages for each hut in which he housed members of his family. Because it was traditional for a man to have several wives and to house each separately and live in a different hut himself, this tax was ruinous. Many of the men had to go to work for the British government or wealthy landowners to earn the cash to pay the tax. This served the British well, disrupting communities and undercutting native traditions and self-sufficiency. The taxes created a vicious circle: African labor built the roads, buildings, and railroads that further entrenched the British in Kenya, and the money the Africans earned was immediately turned over in the form of taxes, which paid for the administration that oppressed them. Rather than a country made up of self-sufficient rural communities, Kenya was rapidly becoming a country of poor Africans and wealthy whites. Traditional ways of life were being replaced by family life in shantytowns near the father's employment or rural life without the presence of adult males much of the year.

Life for the British settlers was not the same as at home, either. For most it was far better. A few were nobles, like Lord Delamere, who sold his English land to resettle in Kenya and eventually became governor of the Kenya Colony. Most settlers, however, were not members of the upper class or wealthy landowners in England. Also, in England the law applied (at least in theory) to everyone equally. In "White Man's Country," or "the White Highlands," as western Kenya came to be called, settlers lived more like the nobility in England, but their superior economic, legal, and social standing had to be maintained by repressive laws, unequal treatment, and armed force.

THE BIRTH OF THE INDEPENDENCE MOVEMENT

The idea of independence from British rule actually began soon after the colonists took over. A quarter million Kenyans served in the British army during World War I, fighting in skirmishes in German-held Tanganyika (now Tanzania) and elsewhere. As is often the case with groups who are discriminated against in their own country, these Kenyan soldiers returned to their native land much less willing to accept second-class status in a society they had fought to defend. They were particularly displeased by the fact that white soldiers in the same war were being given Kenyan land as a reward while the war service of African Kenyans was ignored. As a result, the Young Kikuyu Association was founded in 1921 by Harry Thuku, a government clerk and ex-serviceman.

Thuku led protests against the pass system and taxes, and he even had some success bringing non-Kikuyus into the protest movement. After Thuku was arrested and jailed, a protest began outside the police station where he was being held. To quell the demonstration, the police opened fire and killed twenty-five Africans. Thuku was exiled to Somalia for nine years. Another organization, the Kikuyu Central Association, was founded in 1925. Johnstone Kamau became its leader in 1928. Later he would Africanize his name, changing it to Jomo Kenyatta after the *kinyatta*, a Maasai belt he liked to wear.

LIFE IN HAPPY VALLEY

In many ways the white colonists' lives were similar to those of slave owners in the American South. Plantation owners in Kenya did little of the actual work on the land; this was done by Africans and supervised by overseers. Their social lives in what Kenya colonists dubbed "Happy Valley" were restricted to other plantation owners and visitors from Europe or elsewhere. Thus, life revolved around parties, social clubs, bars, and safaris. It was common for whites to go out for days into the bush to shoot game. It was this indiscriminate killing for sport of lions, rhinoceroses, elephants, and other large game that set these species on the path to near extinction. Later in the colonial era, the airplane became a major means of getting around in Africa; aviators such as Beryl Markham wrote about their experiences flying in Africa, as did author Karen Blixen (Isak Dinesen) about her flights with her lover, pilot Denys Finch-Hatton.

White colonist Oda Johnson with Lumbwa women.

In 1929 Kenyatta went to London and stayed there until the end of World War II. While there, he studied with the renowned anthropologist Bronislaw Malinowski and wrote *Facing Mount Kenya*, a book about the Kikuyu people. This book is considered especially important because it shows that Kenyatta was a remarkable man—a scholar as well as a politician—and because of the record it preserves of traditional Kikuyu life. Kenyatta also spent much of his time petitioning Parliament and lobbying for the rights of Kenyans, including the right to govern their own country, a concept known simply as "self rule" or "home rule." Despite efforts to increase the white presence, there were now 2.5 million Africans and fewer than 30,000 whites in Kenya, an obvious reminder of whose country it really was.

After World War II, returning soldiers were again particularly sensitive to their outsider status in their own land. Sim-

JOMO KENYATTA'S CHILDHOOD

The exact day and year of the first president of Kenya's birth is not known. He was born in a Kikuyu village outside of Nairobi some time in the late 1890s. His parents were farmers, and the young boy tended sheep for his family. His birth name was Kamau wa Muigai, which means "Kamau son of Muigai" in Kikuyu. His parents died when he was still a young boy. As a result, he attended a school run by Scottish Presbyterian missionaries. This was rather unusual for a Kikuyu boy because many Kikuyu saw the missionaries as enemy invaders trying to destroy the Kikuyu traditional culture with Western faith and customs.

At the school, Kamau was baptized and took a new anglicized name, Johnstone Kamau. Kamau was torn between his traditional culture and the new things he was learning from the missionaries. For example, when Kikuyu boys reach adulthood they undergo ritual circumcision, but the missionaries considered this barbaric and un-Christian. Kamau felt uncomfortable going into adulthood without this physical symbol, but knew that the missionaries would be upset if they heard he had participated. Kamau resolved this dilemma by being circumcised quietly in a hospital setting. This is an example of the kinds of stressful and not completely satisfactory compromises young Africans found themselves having to make to exist simultaneously in traditional as well as Western cultures.

ilarly, they had grown more cynical about European attitudes of superiority after serving (and dying) in large numbers in two of their wars. When Kenyatta finally returned home in 1946, he was a national hero because of his well-publicized efforts to win support in Great Britain for home rule in Kenya. The British, recognizing that they would have to give at least token acknowledgment to Africans in Kenya, permitted the establishment of political parties and allowed some representation in the Kenyan Parliament. In 1947 Kenyatta was elected president of the Kenyan African Union, a party whose purpose was to end the color line and establish voting rights for African Kenyans. Not all white settlers were pleased with the concessions. Some saw any erosion in the color line as spelling the eventual end of their lifestyle; in retrospect, they were right. The days of white rule in Kenya were numbered.

White settlers in Kenya had a far more united front than African Kenyans. It was difficult to unite African Kenyans against colonial oppression partly because of their suspicion of each other. Within the known history of Kenya, the different ethnic groups had coexisted fairly well, but they were definitely rivals with a great deal of ethnic pride. As historian Kevin Shillington points out, "In many pre-colonial African societies, there had been considerable overlap between the peoples, languages and customs of a region. Where competition and conflict between groups had existed it was for political power and advantage rather than simply because they were of different 'tribes.'"[7] The European colonists in Kenya and elsewhere had fanned the rivalries into mistrust and hostility as part of their efforts to undercut the stability of traditional African societies. Tribalism creates fractures in society in the same way race or religion does in many Western cultures, including the United States. The Luo mistrusted the Kikuyu, and vice versa; thus, because Kenyatta was a Kikuyu, he had trouble gaining the support of others.

Mau Mau

Divisiveness grew in Kenya after the end of World War II. Whites disagreed among themselves about how to stay in power, tribalism kept ethnic groups at odds, and above all else the color line severed Kenya into two unequal parts. During the 1940s secret societies began to grow among African Kenyans. The most notable of these societies was

BUILDING A HUT
IN A KIKUYU VILLAGE

Jomo Kenyatta's book *Facing Mount Kenya* gives insight into the lives of Kikuyu men and women and shows the spirit of *harambee*, or "pulling together."

Kenyatta explains that when a hut is to be built, a man asks his male friends for help and tells them what materials he needs them to get for him. His wife does the same with the women of the village. The men are responsible for the walls of the hut; the women are responsible for the thatched roof and the food that will be eaten the day the house is built.

On the day set for construction, ceremonial beer is sprinkled on the ground to summon the spirits to help. The circular foundation is marked by a string serving as a compass. The walls are quickly put up by the men, then the men quit work and begin feasting. It is now the women's turn, and men and women sing taunting songs back and forth about each others' laziness and in praise of their own work. When the women are finished, they join the feast. Before dispersing for the night, an elder calls everyone to stand up. He turns toward Mount Kenya, where the god Ngai is believed to live, and chants a prayer asking for household harmony and the blessing of children. The house is then declared open. As a closing ceremony, a boy and a girl light the fire in the new home. The new owner brings kindling to ensure that the fire does not go out because this symbolic fire is felt to bring peace and good fortune. He continues tending the fire, and his friends go home.

Mau Mau. Members of Mau Mau were mostly Kikuyu, who had been made squatters on their ancestral lands and now wanted them back. The aim of Mau Mau was not merely to increase the political power of African Kenyans or to provoke civil war but rather to frighten the white settlers into leaving Kenya altogether.

The Mau Mau rebellion began in 1952 when members set fire to farm buildings and crops and maimed livestock. Members of this secret society also were successful at disrupting labor through strikes. Their targets were not always white settlers, however. Kikuyus and others believed to be collaborators, especially community leaders, also became victims of Mau Mau raids. In October 1952 the colonial government declared a state of emergency. Many leaders of

Kenya's home-rule movement were imprisoned, including Jomo Kenyatta, who was perceived to be behind Mau Mau despite the fact that he had spoken out against their violent tactics. Members of the Mau Mau were forced to retreat into the mountains of the central highlands, where they continued to wage guerrilla warfare for several more years. Likewise, suspects and sympathizers were put into concentration camps by the British colonial army. Nearly one-third of the entire adult Kikuyu population was detained at some point during the uprising.

The state of emergency was lifted in 1959. Figures vary as to how many people died in the Mau Mau rebellion, but the picture presented to the world highly distorted the violence of Mau Mau against the British. In fact, the "terror" was largely inflicted by the British forces, and the victims were almost entirely Africans. As many as thirteen thousand Africans were killed by the British, compared to the eleven hundred Africans and thirty-two whites killed by Mau Mau. Because the British were the ones who filed the stories that were reported in the newspapers at the time, their version of events was not widely challenged. Although the rebellion was put down, Mau Mau was actually a success because the British realized that majority rule would have to come to Kenya and that the repressive tactics of the colonial government would have to stop. Movement toward self-rule began. Africans joined the colonial legislature in 1957, and within a

Police round up Mau Mau people suspected of involvement in the rebellion.

Kenyans raise the "Kenyatta Avenue" street sign in celebration of their independence from England.

few years they were the majority. Many white settlers, seeing a difficult future ahead, began to leave Kenya.

INDEPENDENCE

Two political parties had formed by 1960. One was the Kenya African National Union (KANU), led by Oginga Odinga, a Luo. Tom Mboya, a charismatic young politician, was also one of its founders. The other party was the Kenyan African Democratic Union (KADU). Among its founders was Daniel Toroitich arap Moi, the current president of Kenya. Although Jomo Kenyatta was a national hero, he was not one of the officers of either new party because he was still in prison. In fact, the newly elected representatives refused to take office until Kenyatta was released. When he was finally released in 1961, he was promptly voted president of KANU. This was quite an achievement, for it meant that a Kikuyu, Kenyatta, and a Luo, Odinga, were sharing power in the same party. This boded well for the future of Kenya, for the tribes were working together toward independence from colonial rule.

In December 1963 Kenya achieved independence from Great Britain. Prince Philip came to Nairobi for the ceremony. Great Britain's flag, the Union Jack, was lowered, and the new national flag of Kenya was raised. Throughout Kenya the people shouted "Uhuru," the Swahili word meaning "freedom." The colonial era ended after only seventy years. Kenya was now free to chart its own course into the future.

Kenya Since Independence

For the first time in history, Kenya was now a nation. For centuries prior, the ethnic groups in Kenya had seen themselves as separate entities. Similarly, the whites who remained in Kenya had no tradition of sharing power with nonwhites. The new leaders of Kenya had grown up in a culture that had not groomed them for their new roles. It would be a daunting task to create a new national identity for Kenya that satisfied everyone involved.

Harambee

In 1964 Jomo Kenyatta was elected the first president of Kenya. He saw clearly that the health of the new nation depended on the willingness of its citizens to see themselves not as members of an ethnic group but as Kenyans. "*Harambee*" became Kenyatta's rallying cry. It means "pull together" in Swahili.

Early in his presidency, Kenyatta tirelessly traversed Kenya to introduce the idea of *harambee* as a tool for moving the nation forward. In Kenya, as in many other parts of Africa and the rest of the world, there were already long-standing traditions of communities working together on building projects. Kenyatta told people that it would continue to be their efforts that would build local schools and other facilities in the new Kenya. The government was poor and small, he explained, and could not afford to meet every need. *Harambee* fund-raisers and projects became (and still are) common, functioning, in the words of author Michael Maren, "like a combination of a political rally and a country fair."[8] Politicians gave speeches and pledged personal donations, each trying to top the others. Traditional ceremonies and foods were important parts of the festivities. It was an exciting time as people began to get used to the idea of being Kenyans, not just members of a tribe, governed by Africans they had elected.

Jomo Kenyatta, Kenya's first president.

One of Kenyatta's first steps had been to choose Oginga Odinga, a Luo, as his vice president, and Tom Mboya, a younger Luo considered to be a potential future president, as one of his cabinet ministers. Kenyatta used these appointments to allay fears that he would favor his own people, the Kikuyu. Kenyatta's political party, the Kenyan African National Union (KANU), was comprised primarily of Kikuyu and Luo, the two most numerous and powerful ethnic groups in Kenya. The Kenyan African Democratic Union (KADU), the second party, was a coalition of the other ethnic groups. Under some pressure, KADU was convinced to dissolve and be absorbed into KANU. This was meant to demonstrate that everyone could be part of one team and work out differences together. Daniel Toroitich arap Moi, the current president of Kenya, was one of the KADU leaders who was brought into Kenyatta's leadership circle through this consolidation of the parties. Kenya thus became a one-party country; although the initial motive may have been a good one, the one-party system would cause problems in the years to come.

WHITE KENYANS AFTER INDEPENDENCE

Kenyatta realized that Kenya's whites were important to the new nation as well. Many whites had left Kenya in the years leading up to independence, but many others, particularly those born in Kenya, stayed because they considered Kenya their home. Their loyalty to the land would, Kenyatta thought, make them willing to work with Africans to build a new country. White Kenyans, despite the circumstances under which they had gotten the land, had in time established themselves as good managers of it, and they were far more educated and experienced politically than African Kenyans. Kenyatta saw that fair treatment of white Kenyans in the aftermath of colonial rule was a better policy than taking revenge for African suffering at British hands.

The vast estates of the white Kenyans remained a controversial issue and proved to be a stumbling block to national unity. Africans wanted the land back, but whites argued that simply confiscating it was not fair. They contended that the land now had buildings, larger planted acreage, new and successful crops such as coffee, and other improvements that had been made by the white settlers. Africans countered by arguing that their labor had been exploited to make these improvements, and it was their turn to receive some benefit from the results. A potentially violent clash had been averted shortly before independence when an agreement was reached for the government of Kenya to purchase the land from the whites. To finance this endeavor, Kenya borrowed money from the British government. White plantations were then broken up and distributed to Africans.

Kenyatta worked hard to bring the white settlers who remained in Kenya into political life. His plan was to "Africanize" Kenya slowly, replacing whites with African Kenyans as soon as they developed the needed expertise. Before this time, African Kenyans had been denied the opportunity to go into professions or to serve at the highest levels of government. Few had received high-school diplomas, much less university educations. Kenyatta reasoned that the nation was better off using white expertise than ignoring it, but not everyone agreed. Not too long after Kenyatta took power, a mutiny broke out against him because of his perceived affiliations with white Kenyans. The power struggle had to be put down using British troops. Kenyatta's willingness to resort to force against his own people undercut his credibility both as a leader and as a builder of a democratic, free, African Kenya.

EARLY OPPOSITION TO KENYATTA

The sincerity of Kenyatta's call for *harambee* was questioned almost immediately by others, especially Luo, including Oginga Odinga. Odinga complained about what he perceived as insufficient progress toward Africanization and too much emphasis on adopting Western capitalism instead of a broader, more socialist agenda. Odinga felt that Kenyatta was turning himself and some of his Kikuyu friends into African versions of the colonists. In his book *Not Yet Uhuru*, Odinga portrayed Kenyatta as being more interested in entering the white social world and using his power to enrich his friends and himself than he was in fashioning a democracy and a better world for everyone in Kenya. Odinga and others also worried that Kenyatta's emphasis on attracting foreign investors would result in foreign corporations becoming the real powers in Kenya. Shortly after Kenya achieved independence, Hilton, Firestone, Union Carbide, and Del Monte all set up operations in Kenya.

Kenyatta disagreed that the presence of Western corporations in Kenya might spell problems later. The country did not have many exportable natural resources like precious gems, metals, and minerals, as did many other African countries, and it needed a broader base for its economy than the few agricultural products it was able to export. He knew that a country that relies only on crops to sustain itself is always at risk of disaster if the crops fail, which they are bound to do from time to time because of floods, drought, or plant diseases. A stable, prosperous Kenya would need more than tea and coffee.

The rift between Odinga and Kenyatta continued to grow, especially as it became clear that Kenyatta was guilty of some of what Odinga charged. Personally, Kenyatta was growing very wealthy. He was accepting bribes for political favors and kickbacks from foreign investors. He shared the opportunity for personal gain primarily with a handful of Kikuyu, who were coming to be seen as the nation's new elite. Kenyatta's critics began to say that the term *self-help* had come to mean "help yourself."

Overall, though, Kenyatta did seem to be leading his country into a better future. All around the country communities were pulling together to build schools, hospitals, and other

Oginga Odinga favored Africanization over Western capitalism.

public facilities, using donations and their own labor. Kenya's reputation abroad was also good, leading to increased investment and huge allocations of foreign aid from the United States and other countries. Both Kenya and Jomo Kenyatta were used as symbols of what an independent Africa might achieve.

DICTATORSHIP AND VIOLENCE

Unable to tolerate the path that Kenya was taking toward "Kikuyization" and Western-style capitalism, Odinga began speaking out more openly and was expelled from KANU. He formed his own party, based on socialist principles, and looked for support from the Soviet Union. Fearing overthrow, Kenyatta arrested Odinga and banned all other parties in Kenya. From that time forward, Kenyatta's image became much

Tom Mboya was killed by an assassin's bullet in 1969.

more complex. He was affectionately called "Mzee," meaning "old, wise one," and was viewed as the one person most responsible for Kenya's independence; at the same time, though, he was also perceived as a dictator who would do whatever it took to stay in power.

Whenever a person or a party rules by force, enemies are created where they might not be otherwise. Once Odinga, the Luo champion, had been arrested and thrown out of the ruling, and only, party, many Luo became disenchanted with Kenyatta and KANU. According to Blaine Harden, "In independent Kenya's first fifteen years, the Kikuyu grew rich and the Luo grew restless."[9] The Luo began looking to the future and felt they had a good chance to elect Tom Mboya, a Luo, as the next president. However, Mboya was murdered in 1969. A Kikuyu was tried and hung for the crime, but some feel the rush to blame Mboya's murder on the Kikuyu may have made a scapegoat of an innocent man. One theory about the assassination is that the Kikuyu would not tolerate a Luo being president, and Mboya was killed to keep that from happening.

Ethnic conflict escalated following the Mboya assassination. Kenyatta went to Kisumu, in the heart of Luoland, to open a hospital and was forced to share the stage with Odinga, a Luo national hero. The audience booed Kenyatta,

TOM MBOYA

On a little island in Lake Victoria is a small white-domed mausoleum housing a gravestone that reads

THOMAS JOSEPH MBOYA
August 15, 1930–July 5, 1969
"Go and fight like this man
Who fought for mankind's cause
Who died because he fought
Whose battles are still unwon!"

It is the birthplace and final resting place of a young man who, for many Kenyans, seemed to represent the best hope for the new nation of Kenya. Tom Mboya was a handsome, charismatic political leader who rose to prominence through his involvement with the trade unions of Kenya. Mboya was perceived as the person most likely to be able to transcend ethnic loyalties, particularly between the Luo and the Kikuyu. Although Luo, Mboya was able to gain the support of many Kikuyu and others because they identified with his rural, working-class roots. Also, as a young man he appealed to a different and wider group of potential voters than had Kenyatta, Odinga, and other members of the first generation of Kenyan freedom fighters. By the late 1960s, Mboya was widely felt to be the likely second president of Kenya, after Kenyatta.

Tom Mboya was gunned down in Nairobi in 1969, sparking rioting and demonstrations that took forty more lives. A Kikuyu was tried and executed for the crime, but sentiments even thirty years later remain high, much as they do in the United States about the murders of the Kennedys and Martin Luther King Jr. in the same decade. Evidence of the enduring feelings of Kenyans towards Tom Mboya are the number of facilities, such as schools, that are named after him, particularly in the Lake Victoria area.

and it was reported that Kenyatta turned to Odinga and said he would crush him. As Kenyatta's motorcade drove off, locals began throwing stones at the cars. Kenyatta's bodyguards opened fire. At least eleven people were killed and seventy-eight were wounded.

In March 1975 Kenyans were stunned by another murder, this time of J. M. Kariuki. A critic of Kenyatta, Kariuki was a member of Parliament and an assistant minister. He was very popular, particularly among the poor people of Kenya, and was talked about as a possible future president, much as Tom Mboya had been. He was abducted by the police and killed. His body was left out in a field for hyenas to eat, and his facial features had been destroyed by acid. The murder caused many within KANU to voice their dissent against the tactics of Kenyatta, but anyone who did so was forced to resign from KANU, and their political career, at least for the time being, was over.

Kenyatta's hold on power remained strong, though, partly because he ruthlessly suppressed dissent but also because he was, and still is, thought of as a great figure in Kenyan history. He had led Kenya to independence and set it on the road to becoming a modern nation. Through *harambee*, he encouraged local communities to help themselves rather than expect all their needs to be met by the government. He established a strong personal and national image throughout the world, and it was hard to imagine Kenya without him. Kenyans who opposed his tactics were resigned to waiting until he died to make changes.

TRANSFER OF POWER

On August 23, 1978, Jomo Kenyatta died in his sleep. He was one of the wealthiest men in the world and one of only a handful of African leaders to have achieved international fame. Mzee's passing was mourned, but violence did not erupt. Likewise, the transition to his vice president, Daniel Toroitich arap Moi, was peaceful. Under Kenyan law, the vice president assumes power only for ninety days, after which an election is held. Although many Kenyans did not believe that Moi was sufficiently well known or respected to win the election, he became the second president of Kenya. He still holds that position today.

When Daniel Toroitich arap Moi (*arap* means "son of") assumed the presidency, his name was not even known by most Kenyans. He had not been perceived as being politically ambitious or even as being particularly bright; thus, he had seemed a far safer choice for vice president to Kenyatta than Odinga had turned out to be. Moi was neither Kikuyu nor Luo, a fact that many felt was his main qualification to be vice president. Moi was part of the Tugen, a small group within the Kalenjin, itself one of the smaller, relatively

*Daniel Toroitich
arap Moi assumed
the presidency after
Kenyatta's death.*

Daniel Toroitich arap Moi assumed the presidency after Kenyatta's death.

powerless ethnic groups in Kenya. Many Kenyans were pleased that his ethnic background gave him no strong base for support, which meant that he would have to build coalitions and consensus to remain in power.

A former mission schoolteacher with a rather low-profile but long-standing role in the fight for independence, Moi launched into a public relations campaign to paint his presidency as a vast improvement over the dictatorship and elitism of Kenyatta and his Kikuyu friends. Moi promised new land distribution programs, an end to government corruption, and release of political prisoners. Initially he delivered on all three. As time passed, however, it became clear that he had simply substituted Kenyatta's shortcomings with his own. Moi's government quickly surpassed the corruption of Kenyatta's. Friends made rich by Moi's economic schemes quickly were dubbed *wabenzi*, after their vehicle of choice, the Mercedes Benz. Kickbacks, between 5 to 10 percent under Kenyatta, escalated to as much as 25 percent under Moi. "Corruption," according to Blaine Harden, "was an essential counterpoint to a lack of real popularity,"[10] and Moi relied on it to strengthen his lackluster leadership and personality.

In 1982 a military coup to topple Moi was attempted but quickly suppressed. Moi used the coup as a rationale for cracking down on opposition. The University of Nairobi was closed for a time, churches that opposed him were shut down, and Moi claimed the right to fire judges whose

THE OTIENO FUNERAL

President Moi is widely perceived as fanning hostility between the Kikuyu and the Luo as a way of deflecting anger away from himself and thus holding on to power. An example of his role in creating unrest occurred during the controversy surrounding the Otieno funeral.

S. M. Otieno was a Nairobi lawyer and a modern Luo who was married to a modern Kikuyu, Virginia Wambui. Otieno made it clear by his words and lifestyle that he did not want to be buried in his birthplace, as was Luo custom, but rather on his land outside Nairobi. When his relatives came to claim his body for burial, Wambui objected and the case ended up in court. Wambui was perceived by the Luo as a "bad woman." She had a career, was a women's rights advocate, and had several children out of wedlock before meeting Otieno. But most of all, she was a Kikuyu.

Wambui laughed out loud during the trial when Luo elders explained their belief that a Luo unburied in the traditional way would haunt his village and cause disaster. Increasingly, Wambui's behavior, values, and personality became the real issue at trial. Nine pages of the judge's written verdict criticized her personally, and he ruled in favor of the Luo. The badly decomposed corpse was finally given a traditional burial in Luoland.

For months, the trial was headline news in Kenya; papers sold out by midmorning and there was talk of little else in the coffeehouses and bars. The conflict between traditional and modern ways had never seemed quite so clearly illustrated. Still, lawyers in Kenya privately grumble that no verdict ever comes in that is against the wishes of the president, and Moi had handpicked the judge in the case. To Moi, a Luo win was best because the Luo are "underdogs" in Kenya, and a verdict against them might have angered them enough to rebel openly against him. Because of Wambui's rejection of traditional Kikuyu ways and the generally more casual Kikuyu attitude toward burials, it was clear that a verdict for the Luo would not anger the Kikuyu as much as a Kikuyu verdict would anger the Luo. Few Kenyans were surprised that the Otieno verdict did not seem to be in line with the facts of the case, nor were they surprised when the Luos' relatively unknown lawyer was soon appointed by Moi to the highest court in Kenya.

decisions he did not like. Although KANU had been the only party with any power since independence, Moi outlawed other parties altogether. Over the next few years he also eliminated secret ballots, forcing votes to be registered by requiring voters to stand in lines behind the symbol for the candidate of their choice. Opposition candidates were made to deliver their qualifying papers in person, and they often had them snatched from their hands before they could file them. Election dates were suddenly changed so that people traveling for holidays would be caught away from the community in which they were registered to vote.

Because of unusual provisions in Kenya's constitution, the president has the power to appoint most of the positions with any real power, all the way down to local authorities, without the approval of the legislature or the electorate. For this reason, it is difficult to oppose Moi without losing one's job. Because there is only one party, being expelled from KANU means that a person is not likely to win election. Likewise, since Moi and his closest advisers select KANU-approved candidates, it is easy to understand why the legislature tends to approve everything he does.

Opposition to Moi does exist, but it is suppressed quickly and ruthlessly, as it was under Kenyatta. Charles Rubia, a member of Parliament who spoke out in 1987 in opposition to queuing (standing in line to vote), was shouted and stomped down by fellow legislators and arrested. He lost his seat in a rigged election the next time he ran. His fate is nothing compared to that of Robert Ouko, the Minister of Foreign Affairs and International Cooperation, who was widely thought to be a possible third president of Kenya. In 1990, after Ouku threatened to expose corruption in Moi's government, his body was found horribly burned, with broken bones and a gunshot wound to the head. The death, amazingly, was first ruled a suicide. Moi eventually gave in to pressure to investigate Ouko's death but the inquiry was suddenly stopped when several of Moi's aides were implicated. The murder remains unsolved today.

Demonstrations are also brutally put down. In July 1997, before a national election, students, civic groups, church leaders, and opposition politicians demonstrated in Nairobi for constitutional reforms. They were teargassed, shot, and clubbed by police. Eleven people died. Riot police followed

Demonstrators in Nairobi seek constitutional reforms.

demonstrators into Nairobi's All Saints' Cathedral, where people at prayer, who were not even in the demonstration, were teargassed and beaten bloody. Such violence is commonplace in Kenya today.

DISSENSION AND DISUNITY

Moi has also fanned ethnic distrust and dislike, particularly among the Kikuyu and Luo. According to journalist Blaine Harden, "While Moi wants the Kikuyu and Luo to admire and respect (or at least fear) him, he does not want the two tribes to admire and respect each other."[11] If they did, their combined strength might be enough to bring down Moi. Many young Kenyans, as well as others who have lived most of their lives in cities away from the daily influence of the customs of their ethnic groups, feel that overcoming tribalism is critical to Kenya's future. They are saddened and distressed by the fact that Moi has kept the two biggest tribes at each other's throats in order to maintain his power.

Newspapers are free to fan ethnic hostility, but those that embarrass the Moi administration are shut down. The administration also controls radio and television broadcasts within Kenya. With the development of the Internet, it has become easier for Moi's opponents to leak information about what is really happening in Kenya. Today, via the Internet, a number of East African and Kenyan news services share information with the outside world about events and public opinion in Kenya. It is clear that Moi is widely disliked, and it often seems as if he is about to be brought down by whatever new crisis arises, such as the teachers' strike in late 1998, but he always manages to stay in power. Born in 1924, Moi is now in his seventies. As with Kenyatta, Kenyans apparently have resigned themselves to the idea that he will only be removed from office when he dies. After winning reelection in 1997, Moi said that he would leave office after this new term because he wishes to go into missionary work in his old age, but it remains to be seen whether he will do either thing.

PRESENT-DAY PROBLEMS

Kenya has declined under Moi's rule. The negative impact of tribalism and government corruption are clear, but they are not the only issues troubling Kenya today. The birthrate in Kenya is one of the world's highest. The population, estimated at approximately 29 million in 1998, is projected to nearly double in the next twenty years. Birth-control programs have not been effective because large families are valued in cultures that see strength in numbers and need many hands to do the work of the family and community. The ris-

Prostitutes seek tests for HIV, which is increasing in Kenya.

MATATUS

Kenya is a poor country by Western standards, but its people show innovative ways of helping each other and of making some money in the process. In all but the most urban areas, *matatus*, the Kenyan term for jitney cabs, are the most common way for people to get from one town to another. *Matatus* are a cross between public and private transportation. A person who owns a truck or some other large vehicle outfits it with wooden seats and drives between different locations, stopping at informally established places to pick up and drop off passengers, who pay the owner of the *matatu* for the ride. The system is quite regular; people generally do not have to wait long for a *matatu* to come by, except in remote areas. *Matatu* service is not formally organized like a bus company, which has a schedule and employees. Likewise, there are no minimum standards for the vehicles. Long rides on the *matatu*'s wooden seats, especially in remote or rainy parts of Kenya where roads may not be paved or may be deeply rutted, can be excruciating. Breakdowns are common, and passengers learn to live with long waits, because the alternative for most is not to travel at all.

ing numbers of Kenyans are not being offset by gains in ability to grow crops to feed them. Most of Kenya is not suitable for crops, and the arable land is already being cultivated.

Women are poorly treated in rural Kenya, doing about 80 percent of the agricultural work that sustains their families as well as all of the work of bearing and rearing those families. Women lack many of the legal rights of men and are frequently abused. Clitoridectomy, or female circumcision, which is now banned or at least strongly denounced in most of the world, is still fairly routine in Kenya.

Diseases, particularly AIDS, have hit Kenya hard. Vaccination programs have been effective against some diseases, such as sleeping sickness and malaria, and life expectancy is better than in some other African countries, but at fifty-four years, it is still low by Western standards. Tourism, especially safaris, the largest source of income for Kenya, has been badly hurt by the AIDS epidemic as well as by stories of lawlessness in the game parks. Drug use is high, especially among city dwellers.

Camels bring a mobile library to rural Kenyans who are often isolated by impassable roads.

Kenya's educational system is also in crisis. Widespread cheating scandals and years of questionably qualified educators have undercut the value of a Kenyan diploma. Many critics wonder whether Kenya's educational system is suitable for a poor country, feeling that more emphasis should be placed on practical, vocational education than on the more rounded education that Kenyan children now are supposed to be receiving. Others disagree. At any rate, with the skyrocketing birthrate, even turning out seven thousand new teachers per year, which Kenya now does, cannot keep up with demand. Political leaders are often not well educated and are suspicious of those who are, especially if their education has been in a Western country such as Great Britain. Consequently, the best educated are generally excluded from decision making about the future of Kenya, and future generations of leaders may be worse educated than those who preceded them.

Because of the now-common perception that Kenya is being poorly run by a corrupt government, international corporations are much less interested in investing in Kenya. With their profit margin eaten up by kickbacks, they know it is potentially ruinous to open a plant, a hotel, or any other business in Kenya. Likewise, foreign aid has been less forthcoming because so much of it is stolen in graft by political insiders that what little is left is unable to improve the lives of the people.

A Hopeful Note

Kenya has clearly fallen on hard times, but the picture is not entirely bleak. Blaine Harden says that, "in comparison to its East African neighbors, Kenya is an island of sanity." According to Harden, "Beyond the trimmed hedges, flowered gardens and security services of the moneyed elite, the wanachi, or common folk, have a leg up on most Africans."[12]

The poor are just as poor as they are elsewhere, but at least they inhabit a country that is able to provide some services to make life easier. Author Dennis Boyles makes the same point: "In Kenya . . . things actually work—including the light switches, the postal service, the economy and a reasonably high proportion of the adult population."[13] Vehicles run, schools are open, telephones work, store shelves are stocked with goods, and hospitals have medicines and beds. Though by American standards, living conditions are low for the average Kenyan, they are still better than in much of Africa.

The human and economic resources that Kenya needs to solve its problems are within its grasp. According to Harden, "Kenya is an African nation that has an opportunity not to unravel. But each day, as the population grows, as Moi's rot spreads, the window of opportunity closes."[14]

6

THE ARTS
IN KENYA TODAY

As elsewhere in Africa, the arts in Kenya are based on long-standing cultural traditions. The most exciting aspect of African art and music is its blending of old and new in a refreshing and lively way. The creative energy of the African arts has put them in the forefront of world culture today. Artists such as Paul Simon and Peter Gabriel have used African musicians in their recent recordings and have brought African vocalists and instrumental styles into their music. In visual arts such as jewelry and sculpture, Africans have shown ingenuity in the way they incorporate available new products into ancient styles or create new art forms that still seem somehow traditional.

Kenya, however, is not generally considered to be one of the great artistic powerhouses on the African continent. The Congo basin and Mali are better known for their music, and Nigeria and South Africa are better known for their literature. Likewise, sculpture from Zimbabwe and jewelry from North Africa are better known than their Kenyan counterparts. This secondary status may be changing, though. The National Museum of Nairobi, for instance, has a special gallery and studio space for emerging artists. Nairobi is also renowned for having some of the best recording studios in all of Africa. In Kenya, stone and wood carving are also being revitalized in contemporary styles and forms. World interest in African art forms has exploded in the last decade, creating broader markets and increased interest among more educated Kenyans in encouraging specifically Kenyan art.

EARLY FOREIGN INFLUENCES ON THE ARTS

In a way, the history of African arts over the millennia has always been about the destruction of some art forms by the culture of invaders, whether it be Bantus supplanting bush-

men or Europeans supplanting the Kikuyu. The existence, or nonexistence, of particular artistic styles are one of the ways anthropologists trace movements of ethnic groups in the period prior to written or oral history. Even small shards of pottery or pieces of hammered and shaped metal can give evidence by their design and style as to who was present or absent at a given archaeological site.

A blending of musical styles can be heard in the music of Paul Simon and South African guitarist Ray Phiri.

Along the coast, Arab influence gave an Islamic texture to all the arts and brought other influences from around the globe. Sixteenth-century Venetian trade beads and porcelain from India and China, which were found in graves as far inland as Uganda, are proof of early trade deep into Africa and evidence that beautiful things are easily incorporated into cultures far from their source. Thus, even before the arrival of European missionaries and colonists, the traditional arts of Kenya were affected by foreigners.

However, the first Europeans came with a different attitude than had the Arabs. The Europeans were not looking for things of cultural value in Africa and even assumed that there could be little culture in any land that had not heard the Gospels. The missionaries had a devastating effect on the indigenous cultures of Kenya and southern Africa during the mid-1800s. Missionaries were scandalized by the near naked-

World interest in African art forms has brought about the revival of stone and wood carvings.

ness of the Kenyans (although the missionaries must have sweltered in Western clothing in the heat and humidity). Dancing and all other activities that seemed to hint at sexuality were suppressed. Anything that seemed to indicate reluctance to abandon tribal beliefs or practices was punished. Traditional ceremonies, musical instruments, art objects, and sacred places were destroyed, banned, or heavily disfavored. The patronizing attitude of the missionaries was echoed by the colonists later in the nineteenth and early twentieth century. There was nothing to learn from Africans, it was assumed, and Africans were being saved from their heathen ways by the sacrifices of the missionaries and the benevolence of the settlers who taught the "natives" how to improve their way of life. This attitude carried over into the taking of land and other resources. Jomo Kenyatta is often cited as having said that the Europeans brought the Bible to Africa and taught the Africans to pray with their eyes shut. When they opened their eyes, the Africans had the Bibles, and the Europeans had Africa.

Kenya's colonial era nearly dealt a mortal blow to ethnic cultures. The colonists, by virtue of their economic, social, political, and military power, were able to erode many African Kenyans' confidence in the importance and worth of their own cultures. After independence in the early 1960s, the desire to be viewed as a modern nation caused Kenya and many other countries around the world to adopt Western dress and tastes. Adopting Western culture—its foods, music, movies, and other arts—became the way of showing one's sophistication. To act as if African culture had any value at all was to seem hopelessly out of touch with the times. Although traditional arts stayed alive within ethnic communities, most of the young, and many of the better-educated adults, shunned them as an embarrassment.

THE REVITALIZATION OF AFRICAN ARTS

In roughly the last thirty years, African-oriented art forms have resurged in Kenya and elsewhere. This is due in part to a phenomenon known as Afro Beat, or World Beat. Because of the slave trade, Africans now live in many places around the world and have had an effect on the arts, particularly music, wherever they are. The role of African Americans in the music of the United States can hardly be overstated. They are central to the development of gospel, jazz, rhythm and blues, and rock and roll. As global communication and travel became more common, people of African descent (and others) were exposed to musical styles around the world that had a distinct African sound. Though Africa has remained fairly isolated politically, recognition of Africa's tremendous contribution to the world's music has been a source of immense pride for the continent, helping to revitalize its music and other arts. For example, the distinctive rhythms of Cuban music originated with the slaves from the Congo region of West Africa. In the past twenty years, the beat has come back to Africa as a strong influence in the development of a Congolese musical style called *soukous*. The traditional beat had never been lost; it was simply revitalized by music from another part of the world. Now, *soukous* stars and others have an international audience, sell out the largest concert venues in Africa, and record in state-of-the-art studios in Nairobi or elsewhere in Africa and Europe.

MUSIC IN RURAL AREAS

Radios and cassette players bring new music into even the most remote regions, and Western-influenced bands play in local bars in small towns, but traditional music remains a vital part of community life. Traditional ceremonies are accompanied by dances, vocal and instrumental music, and costumes. Voice and percussion instruments predominate. Traditional music in Kenya, as elsewhere in Africa, is often organized around call-and-response, in which a lead singer calls out some words that are repeated or added to by the other participants; and by polyrhythms, in which several different meters or beats are going on at the same time.

Traditional Kenyan music is not performed in a concert setting. There is no stage, and people do not watch from seats. Rather, the musicians and costumed dancers perform in a suitable open space, and people generally stand or sit quite close to and all around the performers. Special ceremonies, such as age-group initiations, often take many hours or days; during their course, a great number of community members will participate directly either as singers, dancers, or both. Musicians and the audience interact, and people may leave and come back during the day as their other obligations require.

To traditional Kenyans, ceremonies are important to pre-serving harmony with nature and within society. Even today, primarily in smaller, more remote communities, traditional music and dance are still essential parts of many common

KENYAN SONG LYRICS

Overall, African music has a cheerful sound that is often belied by the words being sung. Though some recent African popular music has been accused of being "bubble-gum," with frivolous lyrics and endless stories of finding and losing love, African lyrics tend toward more serious messages about social problems and making good choices for the future as well as protesting, often in veiled terms, the corruption and oppression in Africa today. In the *benga* song "Wed Today Divorce Tomorrow," Kenyan artist Gabriel Omolo tells listeners,

> In church you make promises in front of a priest
>
> But in six months there is a surprise, you want a divorce
>
> Why cheat on each other?
>
> If your life is a problem, why don't you consult your elders?
>
> Weddings take a long time to organize, while divorce takes only a day . . . .

Maliki's *taarab* song "The Captains" is, on its surface, about two sea captains, but Malika explains that she meant the story to be taken as a description of the way two wives fight over a husband, as well as their own status, in a polygamous household.

> I encountered something amazing, a war on the sea,
>
> A shoving and pushing has occurred, and me, I'm in the boat.
>
> The captains have a war, they fight for the rudder.
>
> They show strength to each other, the fighting captains,
>
> And their rudder is rotten, and they have already cut the sail,
>
> But with all their might, they are fighting the wheel.
>
> Me, I leave the sea, I cannot stand their fighting.
>
> Whenever I think I can see their end,
>
> It will be that the nails will come to be far from the boards.

Music and dance still play a role in many traditional Kenyan ceremonies.

activities, including building homes or planting crops. In these daily activities, the musical element is likely to be individuals singing back and forth about the work they are doing. This relieves the tedium of a job like harvesting or thatching a roof while at the same time it reinforces tradition and community ties.

MUSIC IN THE CITIES

In Nairobi, Mombasa, Kisumu, and other population centers, daily activities are no longer tied to traditional village life, and such things as work songs or age-group initiation rituals no longer have much of a place. Yet the cities are filled with music, spilling out from car radios, nightclubs, bars, and cafés. Some discos play music directly imported from the United States and Europe, and many nightclubs feature Kenyan bands that specialize in songs by Western rock or pop groups. Some of these groups closely copy the original versions, but others put a distinctively Kenyan slant on the songs, sometimes by polyrhythmic accompaniment or by incorporating the sounds of traditional Kenyan musical instruments. Others have gone further and fused Western and traditional music into a distinct and unique Kenyan style called *benga*.

Benga music is Luo in origin. It evolved in the 1950s as an attempt to adapt the rhythms of Luo music to a more Western pop or big band dance style, and to adapt the sounds of two Luo instruments, the *nyatiti* and the *orutu*, to the acoustic (and later to the electric) guitar. The *nyatiti* is a small stringed instrument plucked or strummed like a small lyre, and the *orutu* is a one-stringed fiddle made from the soft wood of a kind of cactus. Other Luo instruments such as the *nyangile*, a box hit with metal rings, also figure into *benga* music. "We developed our style from music played at funerals or the music at dance and fighting competitions," says D. O. Misiani, who is by far the best-known *benga* musician.

A Kenyan band performs in a local café.

"People danced very energetically, following the beats of the instruments. We just took that style and played on guitars the music that those people played on drums and traditional Luo instruments."[15]

Benga music is polyrhythmic, as is most African music. This means that the instruments and voices are each following a different beat. This is very different from most Western music, except jazz; in Western music, the listener can usually tap his or her toes to the dominant beat of a piece. The overall effect of a polyrhythmic style like *benga* is a general sense of sounds tumbling together, although there is usually a drum or guitar in the background sounding out a basic beat to make the music more "danceable." The prevalence of traditional drums and drumming styles is reflected in the term *ngoma* music. The *ngoma* is the traditional drum of Bantu speakers, and *ngoma* is the general term used for any contemporary Kenyan music, including *benga*, that has a traditional foundation. Benga follows a beat like that of Congolese *soukous*, which sounds similar to the way a horse's gallop is represented rhythmically. Italian composer Gioacchino Rossini's *William Tell Overture* (more commonly recognized as the *Lone Ranger* theme) has a similar beat. Imagining fast, rather high-pitched, very melodic guitar licks over the top of the basic rhythmic structure of that piece will give the reader an idea of the *benga* sound.

Taarab (or *tarabu*) is another music style associated particularly with Kenya. The word *taarab* comes from the Swahili word for "enchantment," and the music immediately reveals its Arabic influence. *Taarab* music is most popular among Muslims along the Kenya coast. *Taarab* is sung by women, which is unusual in Kenyan music, but less so in Africa as a whole. One of the most beloved *taarab* singers is Maliki, whose voice is perfectly suited to the style of the music. Her clear soprano voice soars in an independent rhythm and melody over the instrumental background. Usually this consists of one or more acoustic guitars, a small organ, and a variety of drums, although large *taarab* groups may have whole string sections of violins and other instruments. There is also a strong Indian influence on the music, which is readily apparent in the style of drumming. The instrumental background swirls in a typical Islamic style, with a gentle, although relentless, swaying rhythm. *Taarab* is the word used both for the style of music and for the parties at which the music is sung. It is particularly associated with Muslim weddings.

KENYAN LITERATURE

Kenya has a strong oral tradition. Before formal schooling became common during the colonial era and then mandatory during the postindependence era, oral storytelling was one of the most important ways of educating children about the moral values and traditions of their culture. Fables are still popular today, particularly as entertainment for children, just as fairy tales are in Western culture.

Kenyan fables often involve animal figures playing tricks on other animals. In one such story, an eagle tells a whole band of hyenas that it knows where there is good meat to eat and convinces them to dangle in a long string from its legs.

A SWAHILI WEDDING

The month before the Islamic holy month of Ramadan is the season for weddings in Mombasa. Swahili wedding celebrations take place in the streets or small squares of a neighborhood, and all of the women who live in the neighborhood are invited. The only men who are invited to these street parties are the musicians. The preparations and the party itself are all considered important ceremonies, and the whole process takes four to seven days. Many of the ceremonies include sexually suggestive or vulgar songs. The day after the consummation of her marriage, the bride is presented to the group and must sit still and silently for hours, adorned with family jewelry and henna tattoos on her hands and feet, while the celebrants admire her beauty.

On the last day the *taarab*, a special musical celebration, is held. Often it will last all night. The heavily amplified band plays *taarab* music, and as the evening progresses the women start singing along or get up to show off their dancing skills or their new clothes. *Tuzo*, or tips, are given frequently to the musicians and singer, especially when requests from the audience have been performed. Often *tuzo* are given for improvised lyrics that fit the particular party or when well-known lyrics seem particularly appropriate. For example, if a song is a warning against infidelity, a woman might very dramatically offer the singer a tip as a way of sending a message to a flirtatious woman in the audience that her behavior toward other women's husbands needs to stop. Men have their own wedding celebrations, but they are much less elaborate. Sometimes wedding *taarabs* are attended by men and women, in which case a curtain is erected between them.

When the eagle is high in the sky, it asks the hyena hanging directly from its legs to scratch an itch under its wing. The hyena lets go in order to oblige, and the whole group of hyenas plummet to the earth. One survived, and that explains why hyenas seem to limp to this day.

In modern Kenya, the trickster still figures into popular stories, but the setting and characters are more likely to be modern people struggling with life in late twentieth-century Africa. The most prominent writer of the last thirty years is Ngugi wa Thiong'o, a Kikuyu. His career shows the difficult position of writers in Kenya today. From the time of his first

PETALS OF BLOOD

Ngugi wa Thiong'o is the best-known novelist and social critic in contemporary Kenya. His novel *Petals of Blood* is set in Ilmorag, a village in the Great Rift Valley, during the early days of independence. In the passage quoted below, villagers are reeling after a bank has taken over several local buildings. One of the characters, Wanja, has taken money from the forced sale of her bar and meat-roasting center and used it to build a modern home outside the village. In the bar one evening, she makes an announcement that will change all the villagers' lives.

One night the band struck up a song they had composed on their first arrival. As they played, the tune and the words seemed to grow fresher and fresher, and the audience clapped and whistled and shouted encouragement. The band added innovations and their voices seemed possessed of a wicked carefree devil.

> This shamba girl
>
> Was my darling
>
> Told me she loved my sight. . . .

They stopped to thunderous hand claps and feet pounding on the floor. Wanja suddenly stood up and asked them to play it again. She started dancing to it, alone, in the arena. People were surprised. They watched the gyrations of her body, speaking pleasure and pain, memories and hopes, loss and gain, unfulfilled longing and desire. The band, responding to the many beating hearts, played with sad maddening intensity as if it were reaching out to her loneliness and solitary struggle. . . . As suddenly as she had started, she stopped. She walked to the stage at the bandstand. The "house" was hushed. The customers knew that something big was in the air.

"I am sorry, dear customers, to have to announce the end of the old Ilmorag bar and meat roasting centres, and the end of Ilmorag Bar's own Sunshine Band. Chiri County Council says we have to close."

She would not say more. And now they watched her as she walked across the dusty floor to where Munira was sitting. She stopped, whirled back, and screamed at the band. "Play! Play! Play on. Everybody dance—Daaance!"

novel, *Weep Not, Child* (1964), through his most famous novel, *Petals of Blood* (1977), Ngugi's works were written in English and were strongly worded social protests about the varying ills plaguing Africans in present-day Kenya. He was a professor of literature at University of Nairobi, and his works were widely available in Kenya. Some of the Kenyan government's open-mindedness about Ngugi was undoubtedly due to the fact that, although he was writing scathing criticisms of government corruption and exposés of the terrible poverty in rural Kenya, he was writing in English. His works were generally only read by the educated elite, and thus the protests his works might have triggered were not happening because he was not reaching the people who were most hurt by conditions in Kenya. In 1977 Ngugi decided that he would write only in Kikuyu or Swahili. After a presentation of his new play, entitled in English translation as *I Will Marry When I Want*, at a Kikuyu community center with a cast of local people saying their lines in their own language, Ngugi was jailed for a year. Ngugi's work in Kikuyu is now banned in Kenya, and he lives in exile in England. Other writers, such as Sam Kahiga, Meja Mwangi, and Marjorie Oludhe Macgoye (one of the few published women writers in Kenya), have steered clear of such stinging, direct criticism of the government and focus instead on the humor, irony, and tragedies of men and women in modern Kenya.

OTHER ARTS IN KENYA

Western-style painting has been conspicuously absent in Kenya and most of Africa until recent years. Painting evolved in a culture where there were large buildings, such as churches and palaces, in need of decoration. Nomadic cultures, and in fact most of the agricultural groups in Kenya, had no use for such buildings. Nomadic cultures tend to focus their artistic efforts on objects to adorn the body and on other items that are easy to carry with them. It would make no sense to carve a large statue from rock if one had to transport it; it would make more sense to fashion elaborate headdresses or jewelry or to dye cloth in pleasing patterns for clothing. In Kenya, the visual arts are well represented by these kinds of items.

Some of the art worn as body decoration has symbolic meaning usually related to status within the community.

Women in groups such as the Rendille change their hairstyle when they marry and again when they become mothers. Men often wear different headdresses or other identifying marks to show that they are members of particular age groups. Often these changes in adornment occur within ritual ceremonies. In some cultures, particularly nomadic ones, the amount of valuable jewelry worn is a direct indication of familial wealth.

Artistic achievement in Kenya is illustrated by the wide range of art worn by ethnic Kenyans. It is visible in the intricate geometric designs of silver and gold Swahili bracelets.

Tradition and artistic expression merge in the elaborate headdresses, jewelry, and dyed cloth found in Kenya.

It is shown in the simple brass and wire bands and strings of beads encircling the ankles, knees, wrists, elbows, ears, heads, and necks of Rendille women, which turn the whole person into a walking piece of art. It is apparent in the beaded designs of the head-band that holds in place the lion mane from a Maasai warrior's first lion kill. It is revealed in the dozens of thin wire-strung beads, often each of only one color, worn by women of the Pokot ethnic group in a kaleidoscope of color around the neck. It is present in the expanses of *kanga* cloth, cotton fabric dyed in intricate patterns of bright contrasting colors, which are wrapped around the hips or heads of women or worn as loose-fitting shirts or dashikis by men. It is also evident in the Nandi's use in their jewelry of railroad iron, telephone wire, and other items pilfered from the colonists.

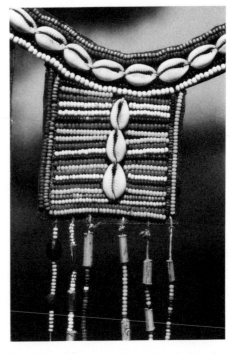

A Maasai beaded necklace represents beauty and simplicity.

The artistic impulses of Kenyans are also illustrated by wood carving, particularly among Maasai and Luo men; and pottery, which in many cultures, such as the Luo, is largely the work of women. Rarely are functional articles left undecorated in some way. Often the patterns make works of art out of the simplest everyday objects. Now, with the realization that foreigners will pay well for African art, many people are turning out decorated household items such as pots and wood carvings as well as other less-traditional pieces for the international market. Some of these products are disparagingly called "airport art," and they are mass produced by people with no particular artisanal skill solely for the purpose of making a little more money from tourists buying souvenirs. Other pieces, which are usually extremely high priced, clearly show the beauty and craftsmanship of Kenyan beadworkers, potters, metalsmiths, and other artists at their best.

FACTS ABOUT KENYA

GOVERNMENT

The official name of Kenya is the Republic of Kenya, and its capital is Nairobi.

Kenya is headed by an elected president who serves a five-year term. There are no term limits. The current president, only the second in Kenyan history, is Daniel Toroitich arap Moi. Under the president are various ministers and permanent secretaries of such divisions as personnel and provincial management.

The National Assembly is the legislative body, made up of 158 legislators elected every five years, or sooner if the assembly is dissolved by the president. Kenya is technically a multiparty system, but the Kenya African National Union (KANU) dominates the government, and elections are generally between KANU candidates, with others standing little chance of winning.

The country is divided into nine provinces.

LEGAL SYSTEM

Kenya has a constitution. In 1998 President Moi agreed to begin the process of constitutional reform.

In Kenya there are three kinds of law: customary law, the laws of a particular ethnic group; Islamic law, the special religious laws governing Muslims; and common law, the national system of law codes used in courts. Common law is the same system used in the United States. It is called *common* because everyone has to follow it (we all have it in common). In Kenya, customary law is used to settle problems that involve two members of an ethnic group, and Islamic law is used to settle problems between two Muslims. Common law is used for everyone else or when both sides of a dispute are from different ethnic groups or religions.

The Kenyan judicial system is modeled after the British courts. Judges and barristers (courtroom lawyers) follow British legal customs, including wearing wigs in the courtroom.

Kenya achieved independence on December 12, 1963, and celebrates Independence Day on December 12 each year.

LANGUAGES

English is the official language of Kenya, and kiSwahili is the national language. Technically, government business and the school system are supposed to be conducted in English, but often kiSwahili is used there as well. KiSwahili is the language for everything else, including business.

Most Kenyans also speak the language of their ethnic group, particularly when they are at home. There are over thirty such languages in Kenya, and there are three language groups.

Bantu languages are spoken primarily in western Kenya and along the coast. The Luhya, Kisii, and Kikuyu are examples of groups speaking Bantu languages.

Nilotic languages are spoken primarily in the area around Lake Victoria and a north-south running band of land west of the highlands. The Luo, Kalenjin, and Maasai are examples of groups speaking Nilotic languages.

Cushitic languages are spoken primarily in the north. The Somali, Rendille, and Turkana are examples of groups speaking Cushitic languages.

PEOPLE

The population of Kenya is approximately 29 million, and approximately 1.5 million people live in Nairobi. It is projected to grow to over 40 million in the next twenty years. The birthrate in Kenya is one of the world's highest (4 percent per year).

There are over forty ethnic groups in Kenya. Actual numbers of each are not known, and the following figures are rounded approximations. Major groups include the following: Kikuyu (22 percent), Luo (13 percent), Luhya (13 percent), and Kalenjin (11 percent). Prominent smaller groups include the Maasai, the Turkana, and the Somali. Others (whites and Asians) make up less than 2 percent of the population.

Three quarters of Kenya's people live in the highlands or along the coast. Population density in these regions, which include the two major cities of Nairobi and Mombasa, is 640 people per square mile.

More than 85 percent of Kenyans make their living off the land.

RELIGIONS

The majority of Kenyans (54 percent) are Christians. Of these, 38 percent are Protestant and 16 percent are Roman Catholic. Another 6 percent are Muslims. The rest (about 40 percent) maintain the traditional religions of Kenya.

GEOGRAPHY

Kenya is divided into several regions. The north is desert, most of the southwest is a high plateau, and most of the southeast and southern corner is savanna, or plains.

Prominent geographical features of Kenya include the Great Rift Valley, which runs the length of Kenya along its western side; Lake Victoria, which forms part of Kenya's western border with Uganda and is the second largest lake in the world; Mount Kenya, a perpetually snowcapped mountain right on the equator, and the second highest mountain in Africa.

Only about 15 to 20 percent of Kenya is arable (suitable for farming). The rest, including all land except the highlands, is too dry most of the year.

Kenya's borders were drawn during the colonial period, using, for the most part, no natural land divisions or territorial boundaries of indigenous peoples. Kenya borders Ethiopia and Sudan to the north, Somalia and the Indian Ocean to the east, Tanzania to the south, and Lake Victoria and Uganda to the west.

CLIMATE

Kenya has two rainy seasons. The "short rains" are from October through November. They are called *short* because they are broken up by periods of sunshine, often in the late afternoon. The "long rains" are from March to May and are called *long* because they are torrential and may continue for days on end.

Kenya's climate is determined by altitude, with the low-lying regions tending to be hot and the higher elevations more temperate. The coast is hot and humid, as are the inland areas near Lake Victoria, which are lower in elevation. The rest of the country is hot and dry most of the year. The higher mountains can have temperatures below freezing, but only the highest mountain peaks get snow.

ECONOMY

Kenya's currency is the Kenya shilling.

Exports include coffee, tea, sisal (for rope), pyretheum (a natural insecticide), fruits, and beer.

Imports include industrial machinery, crude petroleum, motor vehicles, minerals, iron, steel, food, and manufactured goods.

Agriculture is the backbone of Kenya's economy, contributing over one-third of the gross national product.

Kenya's financial system includes a national bank and approximately one hundred other financial institutions such as smaller banks and savings and loans, finance companies, and building societies.

In 1996 the World Bank listed Kenya as the seventeenth poorest nation in the world. However, it is better off than some of its African neighbors.

Annual per capita income in U.S. dollars (World Bank 1996 figures):

Kenya	$350
Uganda	$190
Ethiopia	$100
Tanzania	$140
Sub-Saharan Africa	$460
Worldwide average	$4,470
Western countries	$23,420

Tourism is a major part of Kenya's economy. In 1993 approximately 830,000 people visited Kenya. Its main attractions are the game reserves and the coastal resorts. The majority of tourists are European; only about 10 percent are American.

SPORTS

Kenya is known worldwide for its long-distance runners, including many Olympic champions and medalists.

The most popular sport is soccer, although scuba diving, tennis, golf, and mountain climbing are also popular in Kenya, especially among tourists and the more affluent residents.

NOTES

INTRODUCTION: A VIBRANT NATION

1. Blaine Harden, *Africa: Dispatches from a Fragile Continent.* New York: W. W. Norton, 1990, p. 250.

CHAPTER 1: THE LAND

2. Michael Maren, *The Land and People of Kenya.* New York: J. B. Lippincott, 1989, p.14.

3. Quoted in Richard Trillo, *Kenya: The Rough Guide.* London: Rough Guides, 1996, p. 157.

CHAPTER 2: THE PEOPLE

4. Harden, *Africa,* p. 97.

CHAPTER 3: FROM FOSSILS TO FOREIGNERS

5. Kevin Shillington, *History of Africa,* rev. ed. New York: St. Martin's, 1995, p. 122.

CHAPTER 4: FROM COLONY TO INDEPENDENT NATION

6. Quoted in Shillington, *History of Africa,* p. 35.

7. Shillington, *History of Africa,* p. 356.

CHAPTER 5: KENYA SINCE INDEPENDENCE

8. Maren, *The Land and People of Kenya,* p. 109.

9. Harden, *Africa,* p. 97.

10. Harden, *Africa,* p. 263.

11. Harden, *Africa,* p. 106.

12. Harden, *Africa,* p. 249.

13. Dennis Boyles, *African Lives.* New York: Weidenfeld and Nicholson, 1988, p. 7.

14. Harden, *Africa,* p. 268.

CHAPTER 6: THE ARTS IN KENYA TODAY

15. Quoted in *Africa: Never Stand Still.* New York: Ellipsis Arts, 1994, compact disc liner notes, p. 39.

GLOSSARY

Africanize: To make something African.

agriculturalist: Someone who plants crops.

anthropologist: Someone who studies human societies, either past or present.

arable: Suitable for cultivation (not too rocky, dry, or poor in soil quality to grow crops).

archaeologist: Someone who studies artifacts of past cultures, usually by excavation.

artifact: An object left behind by an individual or culture that is used to gain insight into that culture.

clitoridectomy: The practice of cutting out the clitoris and often other surrounding tissue; female circumcision. It is illegal in the United States and other parts of the world.

color line: A general term used to designate the social separation of one group from another based on ethnic background.

delta: The flat area at the mouth of a river, before it flows into the sea. Deltas are usually fertile because of the soil that is washed down from farther upstream.

elitism: A belief in one's membership in a superior class of people.

escarpment: The long cliff or slope formed when land movement causes a plateau to split and one part of it to slip lower in elevation than the other part.

headwaters: The source of a river or a stream.

indigenous: Occurring naturally in an area.

linguist: A person who studies languages.

minaret: A tower from which Muslims are called to prayer.

oral tradition: The practice of passing down stories and history only by telling them, as opposed to writing them down.

pastoralist: A person who tends flocks or herds.

prevailing winds: The direction from which wind usually comes.

protectorate: Formal establishment of control and military presence by a foreign government over land on which few if any of its own people live permanently. Distinguished from a colony, which is made up of long-term resident foreigners.

rural: Areas characterized only by farms and small communities, as opposed to urban (city) areas and suburban (outskirt) areas.

shamba: A small family farm.

shantytown: A collection of shacks erected and lived in by laborers and the poor near a city or another major source of employment such as a mine.

sphere of influence: A geographical area dominated informally by a single foreign power as a result of trade agreements or practices.

squatter: A person who lives without permission on land legally owned by someone else.

treaty: A formal signed agreement between two nations.

tribalism: Strong identification with, pride in, and loyalty to a group within a larger group.

CHRONOLOGY

ca. 200
Beginning of the Iron Age.

ca. 300–900
Bantu speakers settle in Kenya.

1150
Founding of Mombasa.

1331
Geographer Ibn Battutah visits Kenya coast.

1414
Chinese fleet visits East Africa.

1498
Vasco da Gama arrives in Kenya.

1594
Fort Jesus is built.

1815
British start antislavery patrols.

1844
First Christian missionaries arrive in Kenya.

1856
Richard Burton and J. H. Speke look for source of the Nile.

1860
Source of the Nile is discovered as Lake Victoria.

1873
Slave market of Zanzibar is closed; slave trade is declared illegal.

1874
Sir Henry Morton Stanley proves source of the Nile and crosses central Africa.

1884
Berlin Conference partitions Africa.

1887

British East Africa Company is founded.

1890

Anglo-German treaty settles border dispute in East Africa.

1895

British establish the East Africa Protectorate.

1895–1906

Revolts of Luo, Luhya, and Nandi.

1902

Luo, Kikuyu, and Luhya lands are transferred from Uganda Protectorate for purposes of white settlement.

1903

Lord Delamere, a prominent white settler, moves to Kenya.

1904–1907

Revolts of Kikuyu and Embu.

1904

First forced move of the Maasai.

1907

Slavery is abolished in all British territories.

1907–1914

Kisii revolts.

1910

Large-scale coffee growing begins.

1914

Britain enters World War I.

1919

British soldiers are offered land in Kenya in exchange for settling there.

1920

Kenya is renamed Kenya Colony.

1921

Young Kikuyu Association is formed.

1922

Harry Thuku is deported.

1925
Local councils of African Kenyans are established,
including the Kikuyu Central Association.

1929
Jomo Kenyatta goes to England.

1938
Facing Mount Kenya is published.

1946
Kenyatta returns to Kenya.

1952
State of emergency is declared as a result of Mau Mau
rebellion.

1952
Jomo Kenyatta is arrested.

1956
Mau Mau leader Dedan Kimathi is arrested and
later executed.

1960
Formation of KANU and KADU.

1961
Kenyatta is released from prison. First KADU-led
legislature is seated.

1961
"Million-acre scheme" is proposed to buy land from
white settlers to redistribute to Africans.

1963
Kenya wins independence.

1964
Kenyatta is elected president of Kenya.

1969
Tom Mboya is assassinated in Nairobi.

1978
Death of Kenyatta; succession of Daniel Toroitich arap Moi
to presidency.

1982

Attempted coup by air force officers is put down.

1987

Kenya is officially declared a one-party system.

1992

Newly allowed multiple parties hold first election.

1997

National elections stir protest, police violence. Moi wins reelection.

1998

Threats of a nationwide teachers' strike brings statements from Moi about fulfilling reelection promises, instituting constitutional reforms.

Suggestions for Further Reading

Books

Awuor Ayodo, *Luo*. New York: Rosen, 1996. A good overview of the Luo with many pictures. Part of a series on African cultural groups.

Isak Dinesen, *Isak Dinesen's Africa: Images of the Wild Continent from the Writer's Life and Words*. San Francisco: Sierra Club Books, 1985. This book offers pictures of the Ngong Hills and surrounding areas as well as accompanying passages from the works of the most famous colonial resident.

Kenya in Pictures. Rev. ed. Minneapolis: Lerner, 1988. Very basic, short text.

Kenny Mann, *African Kingdoms of the Past: East Africa: Zenj and Buganda*. Parsippany, NJ: Dillon, 1997. A well-illustrated and informative book about coastal Swahili history and arts.

Rick Ridgeway, *The Shadow of Mount Kilimanjaro*. New York: Henry Holt, 1998. A noted rock climber and adventurer chronicles his adventures and spiritual journey by foot across the game reserves of East Africa.

Tepili Ole Saitoti, *The Worlds of a Maasai Warrior: An Autobiography*. Berkeley and Los Angeles: University of California Press, 1988. The story of contemporary life among the Maasai.

Conrad Stein, *Kenya*. Chicago: Childrens Press, 1985. Good sections on geography and climate as well as other basic information.

WEBSITES

Adminet (www.adminet.com/world/ke). Developed through the auspices of the French Ministry of Industry, this website disseminates information about government and public services in different countries, including Kenya. It contains detailed information about all aspects of Kenyan life and history.

Africa Online (www.africaonline.com). The provider of Internet services throughout Africa, focusing on support and development of businesses. This site has a direct link to newspapers in Kenya and throughout Africa.

RC Bowen Kenya Page (www.rcbowen.com/kenya). In addition to good almanac-style information, the Kuzunga-kazunguka Kenya Webring, operated by Rich Bowen at this site, offers a message-posting service to promote conversations among Kenyans and others about current events in Kenya.

WORKS CONSULTED

BOOKS

George B. Ayittey, *Africa in Chaos.* New York: St. Martin's, 1998. The most up-to-date book on the economic and political crisis in Kenya and the rest of Africa.

Dennis Boyles, *African Lives.* New York: Weidenfeld and Nicholson, 1988. Humorous work on the lifestyles of the colonists in Kenya.

Simon Broughton et al., eds., *World Music: The Rough Guide.* London: Rough Guides, 1994. A handbook of non-Western musical styles and artists, including a section on Kenya.

Isak Dinesen, *Out of Africa.* New York: Vintage Books, 1972. The famous autobiographical account of a white settler in Kenya, first published in 1937, and the source of a movie starring Meryl Streep and Robert Redford.

Pierre Dostert, *Africa 1997.* 32nd ed. Harper's Ferry, WV: Stryker-Post, 1997. This book offers almanac-style information and a brief history updated annually.

J. D. Fage, *A History of Africa.* New York: Alfred A. Knopf, 1978. A thorough history by a noted historian.

Blaine Harden, *Africa: Dispatches from a Fragile Continent.* New York: W. W. Norton, 1990. A well-written account of Kenya under Moi by the former sub-Saharan bureau chief of the *Washington Post.*

Michael Hodd, *East Africa Handbook.* Chicago: Passport Books, 1997. A thorough guide to all of East Africa, focusing on things of interest to visitors.

Jomo Kenyatta, *Facing Mount Kenya.* New York: Vintage Books, 1965. The classic work on the Kikuyu, by the man who became the first president of Kenya.

Michael Maren, *The Land and People of Kenya.* New York: J. B. Lippincott, 1989. A well-written book by an author who writes about Africa for both juvenile and adult audiences.

Ngugi wa Thiong'o, *Petals of Blood.* London: Heinemann, 1977. A novel about neocolonialism in Africa. Ngugi's best-known work. Other titles by this author include *Detained,* his prison diary.

Roland Oliver, *The African Experience.* New York: IconEditions, 1991. This history, organized around themes, is by one of the most noted historians of Africa.

Passport's Illustrated Travel Guide to Kenya. Chicago: Passport Books, 1996. A guide for tourists by Thomas Cook, a noted service company for travelers.

Kevin Shillington, *History of Africa.* Rev. ed. New York: St. Martin's, 1995. An excellent and thorough history.

Robert Thorne, *Discover Kenya.* Oxford: Berlitz, 1993. Another good tourist guide with interesting pictures.

Richard Trillo, *Kenya: The Rough Guide.* London: Rough Guides, 1996. By far the most thorough presentation on today's Kenya, especially the arts and ethnic groups.

OTHER SOURCES

Africa: Never Stand Still. New York: Ellipsis Arts, 1994, compact disc.

Angela Fisher, "Africa Adorned," *National Geographic,* vol. 166, no. 5, November 1984. Article contains photographs of Africans wearing jewelry and other body decorations. It was recently published in book form as well.

Curt Stager, "Africa's Great Rift," *National Geographic,* vol. 177, no. 5, May 1990. Offers pictures and discussion of Rift Valley life and geography, with a small section on Kenya.

Index

Picture Credits

Cover photo: Archive Photos
AP/Wide World Photos, 72, 80, 82
Archive Photos, 13, 27, 36, 37, 40, 67, 73
Archive Photos/Popperfoto, 51
Camera Press Ltd./Archive Photos, 70
Corbis, 7, 11, 18, 19, 97
Corbis-Bettmann/UPI, 29, 68
Corbis/Reuters, 85
Digital Stock, 12
John S. Foster, 86
FPG International, 14, 23, 42, 45, 59, 90
Osa & Martin Johnson Safari Mus./Archive, 63
© Jason Lauré, 15, 16, 22, 24, 26, 32, 34, 52, 91, 96
North Wind, 43, 55
Reuters/George Mulala/Archive Photos, 76, 79
Stock Montage, Inc., 49

ABOUT THE AUTHOR

Laurel Corona lives in Lake Arrowhead, California, and teaches English and humanities at San Diego City College. She has a master's degree from the University of Chicago and a Ph.D. from the University of California at Davis.